Heartaches unto Grace

Heartaches unto Grace

Carolyn L. Keeton

Print information available on the last page.

Rev. date: 05/08/2019

To order additional copies of this book, contact:
Xlibris
1-888-795-4274
www.Xlibris.com
Orders@Xlibris.com
782105

PREFACE

O N A BEAUTIFUL morning in June of 2008, my heart was joyful as I held the envelope of forget-me-not seeds. As I knelt in the fresh soil and prepared to plant the seeds in my garden, spring's beauty overwhelmed me. As the morning air filled with the sweet fragrance of roses, my mind drifted to 1963, the year the army had assigned my husband to Nuremberg, Germany. He had given me roses upon my arrival there during a terrifying blizzard.

As I planted my forget-me-not seeds, I sighed deeply. I thought about how I had prayed faithfully for thirty-seven years, "Forget me not, Lord." My prayer had been that He would free Donald from his addiction to alcohol. How amazing it was that God got my attention with those tiny forget-me-not seeds as I planted them.

On that June morning, I reflected on how peace filled my inmost being. It was such a blessing that after thirty-seven years, God had healed Donald from his addiction to alcohol. I knew that it had only been by *God's grace*. There in the morning sunlight, I thought of the millions of families that had loved ones who were addicted. My daily prayers were with them.

As I sat quietly in my flower garden holding the empty envelope, tears blinded my eyes. Suddenly, I recalled that forget-me-nots love higher places in which to grow. My faith in the Lord had taken me from darkened valleys to the mountaintop. During the years my husband had been addicted to alcohol, I had grown closer to God during my struggles.

Perhaps you may find some of the events in my memoir hard to believe. Please keep an open mind and heart. No spiritual dreams, events, or miracles have been fabricated in my book. I would like my readers to know that my years in Twelve Steps are written about in love and truth.

I would also like to share a secret with my readers. As a Christian, I have prayed since I was a young girl to remember the Holy Scriptures. Presently, I cannot remember them well. Therefore, it is by the Holy Spirit's guidance when I'm writing that my heart brings to mind God's Word. My heart is humbled to be able to have the precious privilege of sharing my story with families among the thorns of addiction.

I want to thank my son and my daughter for their devoted love, the beloved Keeton families, Mike and Kenneth's loved ones, Joan, and her sons, my friend Shelia, and my Women's Ministry for all their faithful prayers. No words can express my gratitude for Bible scriptures from the New King James Version by Zondervan, the New International Version, and the New American Standard Bible. Some names in this book have been changed for privacy reasons.

CHAPTER 1

I N JANUARY OF 1963, a frigid blizzard swept through the Ohio Valley's Scioto County and entrenched itself across the Mid-Atlantic States and the Appalachian Mountains. Gusty fifty-mile-per-hour winds blew so much snow; emergency crews had to dump the snow into nearby creeks. While growing up in the Ohio Valley, I had seen plenty of snow but nothing like that blizzard.

I checked the luggage that was piled beside my bed hoping to find enough room for one more pair of jeans, but there was not. I listened to the shutters outside the farmhouse as they hammered and banged like wooden cymbals. A sense of momentary unease and fear made me shiver even though the coal stove warmed the house.

Thoughts of my upcoming journey to join my husband, Don, in Nuremberg, Germany, tore at my heart. "Dear Lord," I uttered as blizzard winds piled more snow on Lewis Farm, which had covered Great Meadow Road. Faintheartedly, I wondered if everyone in Scioto County had prepared for such a blizzard. The Ohio Valley had been warned, and was prepared for a horrendous blizzard on the way. Now the snowplows were beginning their terrible journeys.

I blinked my eyes nervously as the blizzard winds shook the windows in my bedroom and the snow crystallized upon them minute by minute. Moments later, I glanced out the bedroom window, hoping my faith would keep me strong. I thought of how difficult it would be to say good-bye to my family and friends.

I smacked my lips as I became aware of the indescribably delicious aroma of my mom's apple pies baking. "A little bit of heaven on earth," I uttered, hoping again to find more room in my small suitcase.

I took a deep breath as I remembered a previous tragic blizzard in the Ohio Valley when I had only been ten years old and my sister Joan and I had been alone in our family's brand-new house. Our mom, Edith, had been out assisting a neighbor in need.

At that time, the newly built house on Lewis Farm grew colder from the blizzard. Joan and I noticed that the fire in the stove needed more coal. As we opened the stove's door, a huge chunk of burning coal suddenly tumbled from the stove. Reacting quickly, Joan grabbed the coal bucket, and I gripped the shovel. Although we were fearful, we worked together to shovel the glowing chunk of coal into the bucket.

Then in the blink of an eye and without warning, Michael, our three-year-old brother, got excited when he noticed the coal bucket. "Ball!" he yelled and then kicked the bucket across the room. It landed beside the sofa, and the burning coal tumbled out of it. Instantly the chunk of coal ignited the sofa into searing, scorching flames.

Within seconds, the flames blazed up the wall. The unmerciful tongues of fire seized the new lumber fiercely and made its way up to the rooftop and into the January heavens. Before long, a bedroom wall fell, yet Joan and I continued to fight the fire with a heavy rug.

Although we were grieved and frightened, we fought tirelessly. However, soon we realized that the flames had spread further than we had thought they had.

Joan picked up Mike and screamed, "Let's go now! Let's run to the kitchen window! The ceiling is falling!" As the three of us crawled out the kitchen window with our eyes overflowing with tears, we realized we could not save our home.

When our mother noticed our burning house from the Lambert's porch, she ran home. Joan, Mike, and I had taken refuge in the cellar from the fire. Mother was frightened out of her mind because she did not know we were hiding in the cellar. Moments later, we heard mom yelling, and then her voice was silent. Mom thought we had perished in the fire. Nearly an hour the ambulance arrived. Tearfully, Joan and I spoke to mom hoping she would realize we were alive. With wide-open eyes, she stared beyond us in her own world. We watched as mom pulled large handfuls of hair from her head, in shock and was hysterical as the medics restrained her hands.

During her prayerful month of recovery in the hospital, our mother shared a glorious fact. "The Lord's mercy protected you kids. Never forget that," she said. Joan and I never forgot God's protection during the fire. We still often talk about that dreadful day.

Not long after I had reminisced about that tragic day, I entered the kitchen to check out Mom's pies. She smiled at me, but her words were hesitant. "I know you want to be with Don, but you might not be able to travel in this blizzard today. I will miss you so much when you leave."

After breakfast and Mom's apple pie, I went back upstairs to check my luggage a third time and realized that my jitters were the reason I kept checking. Papa and Mike had left for the barn to check on a newborn calf. I stared out the window at the old tire swing that hung on the huge family oak tree, which had been covered in snow by the blizzard.

I recalled the day Dad had removed the tire from his old Ford truck to make the swing. Later, Dad made Joan and I seat board swings, and higher and higher we swung beneath the big limb. With our hands we grasped the rope, and pretended to be a great eagle which soar the countrysides. Unsurprisingly, when our brothers Kenneth and Danny arrived in the family, the big tire swing seldom came to a standstill.

The huge white oak on the farm was indeed admired above all other trees. I truly believed that nothing would ever destroy its inspiring beauty. I called the huge, beautiful family tree my holy tree.

While staring at the big oak, I recalled a noontime in June spent beneath the big oak when a heavenly experience had changed my life forever. On that day, I noticed a white butterfly passing through the branches of the tree. I watched it steadily until it finally landed.

I thought, *Oh my!* I could not believe that an angel now sat upon the big oak's limb. My heart fluttered unceasingly as I shivered with excitement. I blinked my eyes again and again to be certain that they were not playing tricks on me.

"Did you come from heaven?" I asked. I had hoped the angel would answer, but it only stared at me. It was there for about two minutes. The angel appeared to be a young woman in her twenties. She was so beautiful that it would be impossible to describe the heavenly light around her. Heaven's light showed her hair a lustrous golden blond color and that her white apparel was draped over the tree limb. Then the angel vanished quickly into majestic light, which radiated in a circular motion as the angel vanished.

The next time I saw the angel, I was writing poetry in my secret place in the woods near the barn. Unexpectedly, the angel appeared. She was sitting on a dogwood branch. The angel held a long bright object in her right hand. She slowly moved the brilliant thing, lifting it high into the air as though she wanted me to notice it. I watched mesmerized as the angel's hand moved all around. Within minutes, the angel vanished before my eyes. From that day forward, I believed that angels walked upon the earth among us and could appear when we least expected to see them.

Many years later, I learned that the Bible taught that angels were men but was certain the angel appeared as a woman. *How could it be?* I wondered. I had many thoughts. Perhaps because I had not been able to see the angel's face clearly, I had mistaken the male angel for a female. Perhaps most angels in heaven had long hair. Perhaps angels in heaven were adorned with long apparel.

With sad emotions and a million thoughts, I prepared to join Don in Germany. When I glanced at the pathway toward the barn, I hoped that Mike and Dad would return home. The snowdrifts were getting higher. It was frightening to watch the snow blow in circles.

I thought about how my dad had been such a strong leader in our family. Throughout the years, all the neighbors had commented, "Chaldo is a good man."

Papa had worked during the day at New Boston's Detroit Steel since he had been a young man. This gave him time to care for the farm and Lewis Lake Resort during the evening hours and on weekends. He was a godly, gifted man, who mastered every task he faced. He was a self-made machinist by trade and a wonderful dad but also a workaholic.

Our family accepted the fact that the harvest came first. Because he was such a hardworking man, there was little time for family vacations. Dad harvested the fields at Lewis Farm, spring through summer, believing that all jobs should be accomplished. When my brothers Kenneth and Danny were born two years apart, Papa wished them quickly into manhood and said, "The little plantation will have lots of help."

My parents were steadfast about living an honorable life. Mom always loved to share her testimonies of God's saving grace with others.

In the 1600s, the Shawnees lived in the Lewis Farm's woodlands. When Dad plowed the fields at harvesttime, he often teased me as I skipped barefoot behind him. "Little Foot," he would say, "the spirits of the Shawnee dwell on this land." Then he would roll his black, slanted eyes at me with a smile that everyone loved.

Papa believed that the Native Americans had been treated unfairly. I asked, "Do the Shawnees' eyes watch the harvest or God?"

Papa would respond, "Those spirits rest now."

Mom's contrite spirit was a blessing to the family. She was always gentle and kind. I never saw her angry except once. She was a petite English lady. At nineteen, she had met and married Dad. Together they had built their home on Lewis Farm.

I often found Mom crying and wondered if she really liked country life. Perhaps she cried because she had been a city girl or she was extremely exhausted from caring for the family. I never knew the reason why. The rest of the time, she seemed to be happy.

Mom's delicious cooking filled our home with the sweet scents of country living. Those who feasted on her delicacies never forgot Mom's art of cooking. She was a wonderful mother and a pioneer homemaker.

When I was twelve, Papa decided to take us on a vacation to the Cherokee reservation in North Carolina. The reservation's appearance indicated that many generations had lived in poverty and had had no vision or hope for the future. Their small hut-like houses were in desperate need of repair.

Joan and I played jump rope and other games with the young girls and then toured the reservation. The young native girls did not seem to realize their poverty as we laughed and played happily together throughout the day.

While we played, a chief took Dad fishing and then later gave him a feathered headdress. I never forgot my father's face when the family called him Chief Chaldo. There was no doubt about it. Papa's deep red skin always aroused questions by total strangers, who asked about his Native American heritage. Indeed, Dad was the chief of his family and firmly expressed that goals must be achieved.

My thoughts returned me to the present as I stared at the rental house Papa had built. Sunlight glistened on its icy roof, which had been covered by the blizzard. We had moved back into the small rental house after the fire.

Later, Dad built a new home. He frequently hired help on Lewis Farm. Often, the helping hands lived in the rental house but never seemed to be there very long. Papa always had good reasons when he dismissed them.

Happily, every Tuesday afternoon, Joan and I would greet Mr. Thomas as he traveled through Scioto County peddling his goods. "A welcome sight!" old settlers would comment as they pulled out their long lists of needed items. Mr. Thomas always had a smile on his face, eyes that seemingly changed colors as they sparkled, and rosy cheeks. He was the happiest peddler in the county. Traveling throughout the villages, Mr. Thomas often arrived bareheaded, even in freezing weather. What a sight his bald head made as it shone like sunlight.

As he traveled throughout the foothills of Scioto County, Mr Thomas appeared to be the most outlandish of all the peddlers. He drove his old, beaten-up Ford truck that was loaded with hundreds of things to buy: Kool-Aid, frosty mixes to make ice cream, and pain-relieving creams of all kinds.

One cold fall day, Mr. Thomas arrived in a horse-drawn wagon because his truck had broken down. He smiled as if he owned the world. He told stories that had been passed down from generation to generation, starting with the early colonists. People would listen to him for a long time. They were fascinated by his legendary tales of the Shawnee, who had once roamed the foothills of Scioto County. Then more goodies would be sold.

Papa had a kind heart. He always reached out to shut-in settlers. He would load his old Dodge pickup with fresh harvest and make deliveries in all kinds of weather. Although extremely tired, he would flash a happy smile while passing out bubble gum to needy children.

The gypsies often traveled to Lewis Farm and danced beneath a huge walnut tree. I recalled Papa's remarks, "Let them all camp! Let them all dance!" Dad would then drop his head, which reminded the family that he had once been a homeless lad. Before the morning twilight, the gypsies had already left on their way to somewhere else.

Suddenly, Mom's voice swept away my childhood memories. I hadn't heard her climbing the stairs. "What in the world is on your mind? You seem to be a million miles away." Then Mama had a few more words to say before I left on my journey. "Honey, did anything happen during the year you and Donald lived in Colorado Springs?"

"No, Mom, everything was fine," I replied. I kept my secret from Mom: Don had been drinking after duty hours. Even his faithfulness to church couldn't stop his craving for alcohol. I said to Mama again, "All is fine. I just wanted to think about my childhood before I left the farm."

CHAPTER 2

A FTER MOM WENT downstairs, I thought of Don, who was waiting in Germany for my arrival. Even though I was twenty-one, change was often difficult for me. I was so thankful that Don was a God-fearing man and that his parents had raised him to be a Christian.

I had met Donald at our hometown's restaurant in May of 1960. We fell in love. On September 9, 1961, we celebrated our small-church picture-perfect wedding with family and friends. Two days after our wedding, we left for his new post at Fort Carson in Colorado Springs. More than a year later, Don was given orders to go to Nuremberg, Germany. I stayed in the United States for nine months as I waited for orders to join him. Now at last, I received my orders and would soon be on my way to be with Don.

Unfortunately because of the blizzard, I was afraid to chance a trip to Philadelphia. That was where our car was to be shipped from. It was crucial that I arrive in Philadelphia on the exact day the car was scheduled to be shipped overseas. It was not only important because of the car, but I had to be there to leave for Germany.

My heart throbbed as I stared at the large oak-framed mirror over my dresser, which Papa had bought at a treasure sale. I uttered, "Be strong! Be strong!" *Lord, grant me protection on this journey,* I prayed humbly.

As I breathed deeply in the coldness of the room, there was an overwhelming sensation of tightness in my stomach. What would happen if I failed to reach Philadelphia in one week's time? If I didn't make it, I would have to wait another year to receive orders from army headquarters. There wouldn't be another plane carrying army dependents leaving for months or as the letter had informed me, for possibly a year.

I sat quietly on the bed listening to my parents downstairs expressing their opinions. Mother remarked, "Carolyn shouldn't be out in such a dangerous blizzard." Then I heard her loud footsteps moving toward the kitchen. Thankfully, Mom was packing lunch for my journey. I would need her homemade ham salad, grapes, nuts, and a slice of freshly baked apple pie in that extreme weather.

Papa's voice broke in with a deep, loud pitch saying, "I wish she wouldn't go at all." Then he said, "Mike, I want you to go with your sister to Philadelphia."

My brother assured Papa by loudly responding, "Indeed. Sis will need lots of help in this blizzard." I couldn't help but picture Mike's face when Dad had requested that he escort me to Philadelphia. I knew that Mike delighted in risky adventures. All three of my brothers loved to copy Papa's bravery.

I felt refreshed and sincerely thankful that Mike would escort me to Philadelphia. However, it was upsetting to hear my parents' pleas that I not leave in such a blizzard. Listening to their true feelings was heartbreaking.

I hadn't heard Mama coming up the stairs. Then unexpectedly, a hand rested on my shoulder. "Honey, here is your Indian shawl," she insisted. I noticed that Mama's eyes sparkled with tears as she handed it to me.

"Yes, Mom, I don't want to forget my Indian shawl," I said and gave her a firm hug.

As Mom spoke again, the bedroom light shone through her beautiful auburn hair. It was painful to hear her words. "Honey, please don't worry about us. We'll be okay. We knew that someday you'd leave us again," she said softly and then quickly left the room.

Within the hour, I had wiped my tears away and had said good-bye to my family. It was a moment in life that only time would heal.

The cold morning light grew dim as I followed in my car behind Mike's car down the long country lane. *Don't look back*, I told myself. I didn't want to see my parents waving good-bye from the porch.

Oh, what a piercing pain! I thought as I cried loudly. Deep inside me, there was an ache that was indescribable and unlike anything I had experienced before. Oh, how I would miss my family and my best friend, Joan.

As I followed behind Mike down Great Meadow Road, there was no time for tears. Repeatedly, I told myself that my faith had to remain strong. I rubbed my eyes. "Gracious Jesus, please calm my heart," I uttered nervously.

As I glanced ahead at Mike's car, I felt that his being with me was a blessing. I was not frightened, although the knots in my stomach were painful. I kept watching Mike's every move.

An hour later, fear gripped me, and I became nauseous. Suddenly, Mike halted before we had even gotten to Swicker Hill and shouted out the window, "Sis, I'm going up the hill. Stay right in my tracks." Mike's car scaled Swicker Hill and then vanished from sight.

As I followed Mike's course, my car slid down Swicker Hill. I contemplated what to do next. The second time my car slid down the hill, I realized it was hopeless to try again. Most certainly, Mike would not be able to make it back up his side of the hill to help me. I watched tearfully as cars struggled to get up the steep hill, only to slide off the highway into deep ditches. I was frightened as car after car attempted to climb Swicker Hill.

No, I'm not going to panic, I told myself. I thought I had the answer. I would take the old road through Old Slocum Valley and then go northeast across the old bridge. Enthusiastically, I thought that Mike might be waiting for me on North Highway 23. "Oh Lord, I'm not turning around now," I uttered as I took a deep breath.

For a moment, I considered doing just that. Where had the sunlight gone? How dark the earth appeared. It was as if an alien darkness, which was never to be forgotten, seemed to be firmly in control of the situation. To stay calm, I forced myself to breathe slowly while driving through Old Slocum Valley. In springtime, beauty had filled the valley, but now it was an unbearably frightening sight.

An hour later in dark-gray foggy mist, I spotted the old bridge ahead of me. It was a merciless place. Fog was rising from the Little Scioto River below the bridge in huge white clouds. Very slowly and cautiously, I crossed the bridge and saw no oncoming traffic. Happily, I shouted loudly, "Thank You, God! Thank You, God!"

CAROLYN L. KEETON

As I approached the end of the bridge, suddenly and in one dreadful motion, it was as if I was driving on slick ribbons. The car slid off the roadway and down the embankment into the snow. The car finally came to a standstill on the banks of Little Scioto River.

Below the bridge, my eyes spilled their tears as I recalled the car's plunge down the slope. Fearfully, I wondered how strong the ledge my car was resting on was. Was it made of dirt or rock? I looked all around but saw only dark fog floating up from the Little Scioto River.

I knew the area well, for Papa had once taken us fishing there when we were young. The Little Scioto River was treacherous during winter. I feared that the river must be frozen. "Oh, God, is this my time to die?" I uttered in panic. I feared that if I opened the door, the movement might loosen the branches the car was wedged between, and it would plunge forward.

No, I mustn't think like that at all. Keep a positive faith, I told myself. Before long, an icy coldness came from the river, filling the car with a glacial freeze. When I started the car for heat, I could tell that gas fumes were slowly entering the car. I knew I was in serious trouble. I choked in fear as my body trembled. *I will not panic. I must keep calm*, I promised myself.

Minutes later, I thought my body had frozen and knew it would take a miracle from God to save me. "Lord, I need your angels," I prayed and slowly curled my feet beneath me.

A sudden fear caused me to mourn for myself and think, *God; I've lived but a short life. Don and I have only been married for a brief time. How will Joan, my brothers, Mama, and Papa ever survive my sudden death?* I hated these thoughts terribly.

Then my thoughts turned to my parents. I recalled how they had carefully chosen our friends when we were young. Even the things I had once hated brought a warm comfort to my spirit.

Breathing in gently to force panic away, I slowly stretched a hand toward the passenger's side of the car for my Indian shawl. "Thanks, Mama!" I said tearfully as I gripped it. I quickly tucked the shawl around my body. During the next long quiet hour, I prayed, "Lord, please don't let me linger in the icy river below." I still believed that God would help me.

Suddenly, my legs began to tremble like a newborn colt's as new snow slowly covered the car until it was almost hidden. "Oh, Lord! No one will ever find me now," I cried. Fear had convinced me. Everywhere I looked tree branches wedged the the car in. Snow was packed around the doors. The snow had been blown down to the riverside by fifty-mile-per-hour winds.

Unfortunately, fog from the Little Scioto River was spreading, but the worst was yet to come. Soon the Ohio River's fog would spread into the Little Scioto River and Scioto County. I felt that I was in a world where nobody existed but me. My mouth puckered hard in anger as I realized the grave mistake that I had made by coming through Old Slocum Valley. When I recalled how I had passed no cars as I drove through the valley, I cried uncontrollably.

Soon, I noticed that the car was completely covered with snow. I realized then that no one would ever see my car from the bridge. I prayed that I was wrong. I knew that no one would be traveling through the valley, except for a foolish brave soul like me. Anger overwhelmed my mind again. "Lord, how foolish of me. What was I thinking? I should have known that Old Slocum Valley wouldn't be safe," I shouted explosively as I slowly moved my feet out from beneath me again. I feared that at any moment, the ledge would give way.

Then a tiny stirring of hope gave me peace. I remembered my experience of seeing an angel when I was young. "Lord, you send angels to earth. I've seen your heavenly messengers," I said in humble whispers. "Your Word says that angels rescue us in times of trouble," I uttered to God. Undeniably, I felt a strengthening as I recalled seeing God's angel. Like a spark of sunlight, Lewis Farm came into my mind—the constant flowing of fresh springs and beautiful virgin forests I so loved.

Then I thought of Don's own demons. I wondered if his drinking might had become a serious problem. *No, Satan! I will keep good thoughts*, I assured myself as my teeth chattered constantly. I felt as if peanut butter had been stuffed down my throat. I forced myself to swallow. I knew what might happen very soon: Hypothermia might set

CAROLYN L. KEETON

in. I had almost spent two hours in zero-degree weather. I would not survive much longer and felt certain of this.

Then unexpectedly, I heard a loud voice. It sounded as if it came through a tunnel because it was muffled by high winds from the blizzard. Slowly, I struggled to roll the car window down about two inches so that I could hear more clearly. At first I was not sure, whose deep voice shouted seemingly from the bridge, "I'm coming down. I'm coming down."

"Oh, thank God! Is that you, Mike?" I shouted up the riverbank, hoping he would hear my cries but also fearing for his life.

Mike yelled down to me again, "Sis, can you hear me? Do you hear me down there? Open the door. Crawl out slowly."

"I am afraid to open the doors. The car might slip forward into the river," I shouted.

Mike assured me by saying, "Don't worry, sis. I'm going to remove all the branches and then the snow." As Mike made his way down, his breath was labored and his voice was hoarse because of his asthma. "Sis, after I remove the branches and snow, I want you to jump out quick when I open the door." Within the hour, Mike had cleared away the snow and the branches. *Lord, thank you for sending Mike;* I uttered jumping from my car.

My mind went into a spin because of Mike's safety. "I pleaded. "It's too dangerous for you to try and save my car. Please don't risk your life. Let's go back to the farm now."

I knew Mike had a mind of his own. Once he had made it up, nothing would change it. "It's okay," Mike explained. "I came prepared for this trip. Do you see these big seed bags?" he asked and then added, "First I'll make sure to clear all the snow off the hillside and underneath your tires. I will put the seed bags under the tires to help them grip the ground.

"I want you to stay in my car and get warm. Sis, it will all be okay. This plan will work," Mike explained. Then he said, "Seed bags have always worked for me."

I knew Mike's mind was set when his black, snappy eyes widened. I did not doubt for a minute that his plan would work. Mike slowly gunned my car up the embankment until it finally touched the highway above. The seed sacks worked just as Mike had said they would. They had given the car the needed traction to make it up the steep riverside slope.

"I don't believe it! What a miracle!" we yelled together as I got out of Mike's car, and then we stamped our feet hugging each other.

As we sat awhile waiting for my car to warm up, Mike looked over at me steadily with a serious expression on his face. "Sis, a strange thing happened as I left the city of Portsmouth. For a moment, I felt as though someone was sitting right beside me in my car."

"What in the world are you talking about?" I asked.

Mike dropped his head as if he was thinking and then began to tell me what had happened. "A voice told me to go quickly to the old bridge," he said, rubbing his hands together with a gleeful smile on his face.

Mike poured a cup of coffee from the thermos and drank heartily. Nervously, he cleared his throat before speaking. "Sis, I think this is something. Do you believe God truly speaks to his people? I had no idea your life was in danger. I came to the bridge because I heard the voice. Dear Lord, I never thought you'd be crazy enough to chance Old Slocum Valley," he said, wrinkling his face at me.

I knew Mike was making a point about my bad judgment. He hunched forward toward the heater and poured another cup of coffee. He rubbed his hands again as though he had to think for a minute. "Sis, I need to know one thing. Who spoke to me in the car?" he asked, wiping his mouth. "My, how I wish I knew who it was," Mike said. I would never have thought at that moment that Mike would say years later, "Sis, I'm at peace with the voice I heard. The voice was an angel's."

I looked seriously at Mike and replied, "I believe miracles happen. None of us fully understands the mysteries of God. I believe God sent you to save me. If you hadn't heard the voice, no one would have found me, and you know that. You're Michael my archangel," I said teasingly while patting his hand.

With an anxious look, Mike cut the conversation short. "Sis, are you warm enough now? Once we start heading north to Columbus, some of

CAROLYN L. KEETON

this heavy fog may lift. If we are lucky, we might reach the Allegheny Mountains before darkness closes in."

"That's right. We've a long trip ahead. Don't worry. God will be with us to the end," I assured Mike.

"I guess I need to think that way too," Mike said hesitantly.

Minutes later, I climbed into my warmed-up car. Mike's expression was serious as he pointed ahead of us and indicated that I should follow him. I could tell by the look on Mike's face that he was deeply troubled. Saturday afternoon was growing darker and darker as we prepared to journey onward in the second worst blizzard ever recorded in Ohio Valley's history.

CHAPTER 3

FIVE HOURS LATER, our journey through the Allegheny Mountains brought Mike and me closer to our destination. However, more snow had covered the Pennsylvania Turnpike, and traveling further seemed impossible. We had come a long way that day and had followed a snowplow most of the way. Solid sheets of ice were everywhere. Suddenly, the radio gave discouraging news; The Pennsylvania Turnpike would be closing until further notice.

Mike quickly signaled and stopped for gas and restroom services. What a sight it was inside. People were asleep in booths, children were crying for their beds, and the restaurant was short on food. People from faraway states had experienced car emergencies and now filled all the hotels.

Mike and I were thankful for the food that Mom had packed for us. We would not reach Aston, Pennsylvania, that day. After all, the glacial blizzard had paralyzed the mid-Atlantic and the Appalachian Mountains. It had even reached many places in Europe—as far away as Scotland, I would discover later.

Minutes later, we were on our way. "Keep breathing like you're full of hope," I mumbled. The words flowed from my mouth, over and over. Within the hour, an exit appeared ahead for Harrisburg, Pennsylvania. I could not see Mike's car through the blizzard. What had once looked like green grass on the horizon was now a city of dreadful beauty. My heart was relieved, and I was thankful that we had reached an exit before darkness had descended upon us in the high mountains.

As I entered the city, cars were everywhere. The scene looked like a giant spiderweb. Some of the cars banged into one another as they slid on the icy pavement. I glanced around, hoping to see Mike's car somewhere. "Dear God, where is he?" I blurted out as my heart pounded quickly. *Surely, he'll arrive soon*, I assured myself.

A few minutes later, I realized Mike was nowhere to be found. I thought that he must have gotten lost in the blizzard. My stomach tightened like curtains being pulled together.

Dear Lord, did Mike take the turnpike to Pittsburg by mistake? I wondered. In such a terrible blizzard, perhaps he had failed to see the exit.

We triumph by faith, I reminded myself. No indeed, I would not journey to Germany depending on fate's hand. "Good things happen to those who keep complete trust in God," I yelled loudly.

Suddenly, an unbearable fear squeezed my mind before self-pity chimed in. My car skidded off the main street and into a ditch about four-feet deep. "Dear me," I screamed. Struggling to calm myself, I rolled down the window in anticipation of someone seeing me. *Thank God, it's not a riverbank*, I thought while giving thanks to God jubilantly.

Within minutes, a strong young man stood there peering down at me. "Are you okay?" he shouted above the noise from the blizzard.

"I'm okay," I replied gratefully.

The young man's face squinted as he said reassuringly, "I will call a garage for you." The gentleman's mouth twisted into a smile, and he pointed across the street. "I own that hotel right on the corner. Can you see that building through the blizzard? I'll call a tow truck and then take you to my hotel." Noticing my license plate, he assured me as he waved his hand in the air, "Oh, I see you're traveling from Ohio. Please don't worry. You'll be out of this wicked blizzard soon."

My heart leaped like a frog out of water. I knew that I had to depend on this stranger for help, even though I had promised my parents that I wouldn't trust strangers on my journey.

I wished the blizzard would dissolve into summer's warmth. At that moment, I saw a truck from the towing service making its way toward my car.

I prayed that Mike had already made it safely to the hotel. My mind was exhausted from worry, and my body trembled.

After the tow truck pulled me from the ditch, I followed the young man to the hotel. There, he graciously carried my luggage into the hotel and vigorously closed the door behind us.

In the hotel lobby, a huge grandfather clock chimed many times. I felt every nerve in my body twitch each time its chimes hammered loudly. The young man glanced at me and then at the clock. "That clock has been in this hotel since I was a boy. My grandfather owned the hotel. He passed away four years ago," the young man explained.

I assumed that the young man was taking pity on my situation. Indeed, his grand display of kindness had impressed me. I realized that I should not have feared him. I tried to mute my thoughts, but they would not be silent. "See, Papa. Strangers can be nice," I whispered.

The owner went to the hotel desk and then returned. "I'll escort you to your room," he said contritely, picking up my suitcase. "Oh, by the way, my name is Charles Patrick. I must say, you're a brave young lady to be in such a blizzard. What's your name?"

I smiled confidently, trying to dispel my concern, and then answered, "Carolyn. I am flying to Frankfurt. My husband is stationed near Nuremberg in the small town of Furth, Germany. Don is a noncom army staff sergeant and a medical specialist at Furth Medical Clinic. He does X-rays, treats soldiers who have minor injuries, and goes on field trips with supplies for soldiers."

There was no doubt about it. Charles was spiritually humble and a very good-looking man. He twisted his mouth into an Irish grin and said, "Here's your room, Carolyn," setting my luggage inside.

Charles smiled at me as though he knew my thoughts were centered on my stomach. Walking toward the door, he added, "I know you must be starved. Would you like something special for dinner? If so, I'll have our chef prepare it right away."

Charles's words were beyond my imagination. *A chef will prepare a special meal for me,* I thought uncomfortably. Because of my expression, Charles must have understood that I desired no special attention. "No thank you, Charles," I said firmly. "I'll trust the dinner menu. I'm a country girl who was taught to be thankful for all kinds of food. Thank you for being so kind."

Later, I still felt unsettled, but dinner was waiting. I ate a few bits of meat loaf as the fear that Mike might be in danger gripped my stomach. There would be no highway patrol out looking for him. Charles had already said that the turnpike would be closed for days. The blizzard had paralyzed the town. There was nothing I could do but pray humbly.

About thirty minutes later, Charles entered the dining room while I was eating. "Are you enjoying the meat loaf?" he asked, smiling.

"Yes, thank you," I replied with a hoarse voice.

Charles raised his eyebrows as he informed me of the sad news. "I have checked with all the hotels. Your brother Mike doesn't seem to be in the city. It is hard to say where Mike may be lodging."

My heart raced with apprehension. *Where in the world could Mike be?* I thought and worried for the next two days. "Please keep searching for him. He might be in a dreadful situation," I pleaded with Charles.

For two days, Charles continually searched the city until all hope had vanished. I decided not to phone my parents about Mike's disappearance. My parents could do nothing to help us but pray. I would not cause them worry. They were already stressed about our journey.

On the second night that Mike was missing, I prepared to go on to Pennsylvania without him. I felt as though my heart was breaking into a millions pieces as I worried about Mike's safety.

Throughout the night, I heard voices in the hall as people sought refuge from the dreadful blizzard. Hotels had reached capacity, so neighboring towns were asked to take in those who were seeking shelter. The blizzard had swept through all of the New England states, and many travelers were stranded for days to come.

Later that night in my bedroom, I knelt beside the bed and prayed, "Lord, watch over Mike and keep him safe. Please clear my way for tomorrow. I feel so helpless." I prayed that Mike was safe and had made it to the home of Don's sister. Beulah's home was in Aston, Pennsylvania. She had arranged for us to stay with her. Don's sister Doris would be taking me to the airport.

Despite my fearfulness, I kept my confidence in God. I thought about Don. I knew he would be worried sick about me traveling alone. I wrote on the wall of my heart, *Lord, You are my Shepherd. I'm so out of control.* I prayed, "Please, Lord, protect me and help me."

Restlessly, I stared through my bedroom window. I noticed that the wind was tossing street signs about. I imagined that terrifying moments lay ahead. "Will my faith stand strong?" I whispered.

I imagined how our lives would change if Don was still drinking. Our married life could change like the blizzard outside with new encumbrances, chaos, and confusion.

I folded back the bedspread and prepared myself for a much-needed night's rest. I only slept a few hours because worried feelings about Mike caused me anxiety.

The next morning, the blizzard winds were much worse. I dressed in my long brown wool skirt and boots and went quickly downstairs for breakfast. I could not help but notice Charles's radiant smile as he greeted me in the dining room.

I eagerly said, "I'm leaving in an hour—as soon as the fog lifts," I informed him. "The news reported that the Pennsylvania Turnpike is open," I said and then added impatiently, "I can't believe I've been here two days."

His voice was perfectly composed when he said, "I don't understand." It was apparent he had hoped I would stay a few more days or at least until it was announced that all the highways had been cleared.

Then Charles's face turned somewhat red, and he said, "Carolyn, I've no right to say this, but I feel you shouldn't go to Germany at all. It's too dangerous to travel right now but perhaps later it will be better. Here is my phone number. If you need anything, call me. I will come and help you or send help to you."

Oh my! How kind of Charles, I thought. Charles was kind and friendly to all of his guests, I realized gratefully. He had been a blessing to know. His words had been encouraging and humble just when I had needed to hear them. I never forgot Charles's good deeds and kindness throughout the years.

I observed deep sincerity in Charles's voice when he said, "I wish you wouldn't leave in this blizzard," and then gave me a gentle hug.

Of course, it would be a pity if I missed the opportunity to tell Charles my deepest feelings, so I said, "I wish to thank you for being my friend."

CAROLYN L. KEETON

Quickly, I left the hotel and hurried across the street to my car. I did not tell Charles what my heart truly wanted to tell him. I wanted to say that when God was our Great Shepherd, He would prepare a safe place for us to lodge.

The next day, I arrived safely at the home of Don's sister in Aston, Pennsylvania. Mike came running out the door to meet me. Indeed, he had missed the exit sign, thinking we were going to Pittsburg and not to Philadelphia. He could hardly see the exit sign and had driven nearly fifty miles through the blizzard toward Pittsburg.

He looked as though he had been on a long hunting trip, and I knew he felt as though he had. Mike closed his eyes and nodded. "Sis, I pray the rest of your journey will go well. We will never forget our trip together," he admitted, raising one eyebrow as he blinked his eyes, which was one of his cute habits.

Early the next morning, Mike and Don's sister Doris graciously escorted me to Northeast Philadelphia Airport. Minutes later, I whispered in Mike's ear, "I told you God's grace would be with us all the way."

Mike did not respond to my words. He was so sad that I was leaving. Mike would remain in Aston for one week with Don's sister Beulah and her husband Rudy. The icy roads were still very dangerous. I felt relief that Mike would not be risking his life until all the roads had been cleared in the Ohio Valley.

Mike shuddered, dropped his head, and glanced down at his ranch boots, saying, "Sis, the family will miss you."

An hour later, the early morning sun caused the heavens to appear the palest pink as mounds of ice gleamed like silver plates on the runway in distance. I glanced at the old worn-out army turboprop plane. *Oh Lord, is that the plane?* I thought.

With sadness, I kissed my family good-bye. The noise of the plane starting its engines pierced through the words, "I love you."

Moments later, I went on board and looked around, trying to decide where to sit. I noticed right away that the plane was obsolete. The seats had small cracks from years of wear, and the floor didn't have a carpet.

Its freshly painted interior was a faded-gray color. I thought that if I sat near a window, the trip might be a little more interesting.

Before long, I would find out that flying caused my heart to flutter because I feared great heights. It would be more frightening than stepping on a mouse barefoot or my horse, Star, throwing me into a creek. I thought it was a terrible old plane.

Radiantly, the sun shone over the horizon as the plane lifted off the runway. I caught a last glimpse of Mike waving good-bye below me. Lifting a hand from my lap, I wiped my face as tears dripped down. I moved my head toward the window for a better look and shrugged impatiently as the plane lifted higher and higher. There was no doubt that flying was for the birds. Just the same, I forced a smile and acted as though nothing was bothering me. I covered myself with my Indian blanket and prayed that Don wouldn't be drinking when I reached Germany.

I often thought Don's drinking might have started when he was younger. His life had been very difficult as a young boy. His head and body shook all over, and he had to take pills daily. At that time, it was known as muscle twitching. Children at school laughed at Don. His twitching disorder was healed before I met him.

He joined the army, which changed his life for the better. Later, as a stutterer he entered Walter Reed Medical Center for speech therapy. When we attended the Southern Baptist Church in Colorado Springs, Don's stuttering slowly disappeared.

When I first met Don, words often stuck in his mouth. I would hold his hand and wait for him to say words like *chocolate*. I continually encouraged Don that God could heal his stuttering.

I discovered that while Don had been posted at Fort Carson, Colorado, he had started drinking. I prayed for clarity as to why he was drinking. I faithfully reminded myself, *I must never forget that Don and I will only be what God teaches us to be.*

Suddenly, a tall lady stood up in the plane and interrupted my deepest memories. "I've never seen a hunk of junk like this. This old plane isn't safe," the lady commented firmly and loudly.

Unexpectedly, a good-looking sergeant spun around to face the lady. "Lady, let's not forget it is 1963, and the cold war is rapidly escalating. Soviet aggression is all over the world as USSR engages in proxy wars in the Cuban Missile Crisis. Army dependents with large families are not going on commercial flights."

The lady gave no reply, but her face revealed her feelings of deep disappointment. I agreed that the old plane should not be flying.

I didn't want to think about Don's drinking but wanted to rest peacefully. The plane only had a little bit of heat, and my feet were stinging from the cold. Before long and with uncomfortable ease, I felt my body drifting slowly into wonderland.

After nearly five hours of flying, my wished were granted. When I awoke my mind was at peace about Don's drinking, and I felt refreshed and jubilant. Stretching around in my seat, I noticed everyone was very relaxed. I thought that some of the passengers must be simple folks but perhaps others were well-to-do.

Then another middle-aged lady voiced her concerns, saying, "I've never flown in turbulence like this in my life." Her voice came from the back of the plane. "The plane is jolting about so much, it is causing my son Tom to be very sick," her voice stressed. Instantly, I sensed panic in the lady's voice and struggled to reach her in back of the plane.

"My name is Anna," said the lady. "My son Tom is very ill. Can anyone help him? Tom was born with diabetes. Is there a doctor on the plane?" Anna asked tearfully.

"No, Anna, I don't believe there's a doctor on the plane," I said to Anna, "but I will check to be sure." I'll get the sergeant to check for a doctor and help you." I stood up and said to the passengers, "Please tell the sergeant a mother needs help in the back of the plane right away."

Within seconds, the sergeant appeared, swallowing with difficulty because of the coldness in the plane, and then whispered to Anna, "Madam, it's dreadfully cold. I am going to gather coats from passengers and cover Tom to make him warmer. "We've no doctor on this plane, so we must do what is required to keep Tom comfortable."

I gave Anna my Indian shawl to help out and said a prayer over Tom quietly. "Give my thanks to those who are giving up their coats," Anna told the sergeant as her hands trembled.

After the sergeant examined Tom, he realized Tom was not sleeping. The sergeant whispered in Anna's ear, "Tom is comatose."

"Oh, no!" cried Anna. "Momma is right here, sweetheart. Don't be afraid! Don't be afraid!"

There was little anyone could do for Tom but pray. Instantly, the middle-aged sergeant took control as all great soldiers do in a crisis. "I'll be right here with you," the sergeant said as he comforted Anna.

I wondered about the people on board who had a different faith. Would they be offended if we all prayed for Tom? No one mentioned prayer, so I silently prayed anyway.

I noticed that Anna had four young children and needed help with them. "Anna, don't worry. I'll take care of your children. I'll take your kids up front. There is one empty seat behind me, and I'll watch over them there."

Minutes later, I shivered as I glanced out the window. A ray of sunlight came through a cloud and then glittered upon the plane's wing. My stomach contracted as I realized that there was more ice higher up the wing than before.

"Dear God!" I uttered. *Will this plane reach its destination?* Such thinking caused me to tremble with fright and anxiety. Although the plane was cold, I felt warm sweat as my body filled with fear. Suddenly, I felt overwhelmed at seeing that icy wing. Deep within my inmost being, I felt a terrible foreboding of what might happen on our flight. However, I smiled at the children and hugged them tightly. As I glanced from one child to another, I prayed that they would soon be sleeping peacefully.

Minutes later, a copilot announced, "Things will settle down pretty soon. Unfortunately, the radar on the plane is no longer working. The freezing blizzard has possibly destroyed it. Presently, I'm unable to contact airports. However, if I am right, the airport at Dundee, Scotland, may be aware that we are en route and may expect us to arrive there. Indeed, I feel Scotland is expecting me to try and make a landing there." As the man started to leave, he spoke again, "Unfortunately, we're very low on fuel, but I feel we may be able to reach Scotland with what we have."

Then the short copilot glanced at Anna and said, "Please try not to worry about your son. We're doing everything possible to get Tom to a hospital. However, there is one more thing. Since the plane has no radar, the airports may assume we had a problem or went down." While he informed us, his body swayed as the plane shook terribly.

Why would a copilot tell us that? I thought. As I watched Anna's children, I noticed Tom's brothers and sisters were laughing together. Their laughter showed no sign of fear, and that was good. Then a child's simple faith welled up in my spirit. *God desires a childlike faith,* I thought as I watched the children innocently playing with their funny cards. I was glad the children did not understand the copilot's words.

I could not help wondering, *are souls praying for us to reach Scotland?* I felt as though I wanted to hide, but there was nowhere to run. Of course, the plane could not land on the ocean. That would be the end of our journey. *How could this all be happening in one day?* I thought. I felt overwhelmed and prayed to God that the plane had enough fuel to reach Scotland.

After the copliot's visit, the passengers were quiet except for the children. Finally, at around 7:30 p.m., the plane landed at Dundee Airport in Scotland. It made a mighty shaky landing and skidded into plowed mounds of snow that appeared to be ten feet or higher.

Everyone shouted with joy. Suddenly, the passengers watched men rushing with bright lights toward the plane. The pilot opened the passengers' door to welcome the three men.

"There's a ramp outside the door. Just be careful when you get off the plane. Please attend to the boy first," the pilot shouted loudly.

The medics carried little Tom off the plane first as we all watched quietly. A medic remarked, "We've all been worried terribly, but somehow, we felt you'd try and reach Scotland. We were told there is a snow blizzard like this one also in the United States."

"Can you get the boy to the hospital?" the pilot asked.

"Don't worry. We'll get him there somehow. I've never seen such a blizzard in Scotland before," the tall medic replied.

The pilot remarked, "I've never piloted a plane in a blizzard like this during all my years of flying."

An hour later, happy bagpipers welcomed us as we entered the warm airport. A tall Scotsman spoke up, saying, "All of Scotland is frozen like sheets of ice."

"We bagpipers have been on tour. Been here two days now," the piper complained and then blew softly on his bagpipe. Suddenly, the bagpipers sounded off loudly, playing, "God Bless America," and extending their deepest hospitality to welcome us. A couple of Scots were discussing how the pilot had magnificently and bravely brought us through an unbelievable trip.

Within the hour, a large van took army dependents to a nearby hotel, which was right behind the airport. A tall Scotsman met us to unlock the door, and then the passengers made their way inside.

Once I was inside my guest room, I reached for a small bag that I had packed for my journey. "Oh, my, Hershey's Kisses," I muttered, opening my mouth widely. I was glad I had packed chocolate for the trip. I was hungry for hot food but thankful for a vending machine sandwich, which was given to dependents by a young tall Scotsman.

As I lay down on the small bed, I contemplated what Germany would be like. Would the Germans be friendly? What kind of house had Don rented? How long would we wait until we moved to our quarters on post?

I was excited to explore Germany but most of all, to be with Don once again. As I thought of him, I knew he would be terribly worried about me because my arrival in Frankfurt was already two days overdue.

The next morning, we received good news. God had spared Tom's life, but he had to remain in the hospital for at least two weeks. Later, the van took me to visit Tom at the hospital. I gave Anna a good-bye hug.

"Thanks so much for your help with my children. I'm to remain in Scotland until my husband is notified to join me. It has been so nice meeting you," Anna said tearfully as she hugged me tightly.

Two days after the plane had landed in Scotland, the pilot called everyone together. "We've been here two days now, but tomorrow morning we fly to Frankfurt. The plane is now repaired," he shouted as he raised his hands in the air. Most of the passengers shouted, "Thank God!"

The passengers cheered, but I drew in a long breath. *Lord, must I get on that plane again?* I thought, shrugging impatiently. However, time was too valuable for me to spend it complaining. After all, God was merciful when the plane had had little fuel and had allowed it to land safely. I had to take a leap of faith if I hoped to reach Frankfurt, Germany.

CHAPTER 4

RIGHT ON SCHEDULE, the plane lifted into the sky like an eagle from its nest. My mouth gaped open as I studied the faces of those around me, hoping to see serene expressions. Perhaps if other passengers were at ease, I would calm down. *Oh, ye of little faith,* my spirit whispered to me. I had made a promise to trust God on my journey, yet I shook with apprehension to fly again on that old plane.

The sun shone wondrously, outlining Scotland below and revealing a perfect portrait of a country froze in time. Mounds of snow cast a silvery hue like beautiful huge ice palaces. *What a relief. Lord, bless our way,* I almost uttered aloud as Scotland vanished like a crystal planet. Thankfully, one hour and forty-three minutes later, I would meet Don in Germany.

The flight to Frankfurt was nearly perfect. Thoughts of seeing Don again made me feel so wonderful. He had missed me terribly, and I knew he loved me dearly.

One hour and forty-three minutes later, the plane landed on the runway in Frankfurt, Germany. What a wonderful flight it had been.

No need to fear now, I thought as my heart beat in my ears. "Oh, where's my Indian shawl?" I gasped, searching behind me. Quickly the pilot walked to the front of the plane. Pausing for a moment and glancing over at my seat, he said, "Madam, there's a shawl beneath your seat. You must have dropped it."

"Oh, thank you, sir," I replied. I could not imagine losing my precious Indian shawl. I sat for a few moments gazing through the window before I departed the plane.

Once outside, I noticed I had never seen a winter so frightening. Everywhere, snow and ice were piled high. The piles were up to the windowpanes on the buildings. I wondered about survival in such a terribly cold country. I pushed back my fear as I realized that a new world had opened to me in this strange country. When I thought about Germany, I felt as though I was entering a new world.

Where's Don? I wondered. What a horrible experience not to see his face as I searched the crowd. Suddenly through a huge door, he came running toward me.

"My love," Don whispered, holding me in his arms. "I have waited for this moment." Our tears flowed, and he said, "We were told they had lost contact with the plane somewhere over the ocean."

Don continued, "I couldn't help but think the plane had gone down. I've been out of my mind with worry. I've been waiting here for three days with the other soldiers to hear good news. We were told that airports in other countries had been shut down due to this terrible blizzard. We refused to leave until we knew the truth." Don gave a heavy sigh of relief. "Honey, I'm so sorry. We've only got time to grab a sandwich, and then I must return at once to Furth. I'm now AWOL! I secretly arranged a flight to Furth in a plane carrying laundry supplies."

"What must I do?" I asked as I glanced around at snow mounds that were five feet or higher.

"Love, you must take the train to Furth. I have your ticket. I'll be at Furth station when the train arrives. Don't worry. It will be okay. You'll be traveling through the Black Forest. I know you'll love the countryside," Don commented.

I could tell by the look on Don's face that he was disappointed that he could not travel with me. As Don kissed me good-bye, I was thankful that he had not been drinking again.

"I must leave right now," said Don as he ran toward his airplane in the snowy field.

I glanced around and saw that the train station was right near the airport. I could see it in the distance. I quickly made my way toward the station. I was anxious to feel some heat on my frozen body. "Will I ever get warm again?" I uttered to myself as I wrapped my shawl tightly around me.

I stepped nervously on board the train, and then the conductor seated me in a small compartment. I turned around to get a better view of the station's overpowering structure. Frankfurt's huge station appeared to be an ancient structure.

As I snuggled into the corner of my seat, my teeth refused to stop chattering. Feeling somewhat embarrassed, I forced my mouth shut, but then it felt like I was talking to no one. I felt obliged to smile and nod as passengers passed me. Nodding the head seemed to be a German custom.

Soon the monstrous iron train with its rusty ice-covered frame moved slowly from the city. I remembered that Papa's tractor had often sounded like the old train. It had rumbled like thunder, had sent up steam, and then had quieted down to a lower tone.

Before long, we had left the city and were in the country. I had been on the train for about an hour. I was excited to see that we were entering a forest. "Oh! It's the Black Forest," I mumbled while peering out the window. Everything became darker suddenly. It also looked like every tree was wearing a white nightgown from heaven. Every tree was covered with snow.

From among the trees, a sinister dark-gray fog arose as the train moved very slowly for travelers to view the Black Forest. It gave me an eerie feeling. Everywhere I looked, there appeared to be smoky fog in the forest. As I watched intensely, I became convinced that no one would want to explore the Black Forest during winter.

When the train approached the Rhine-Main-Danube Canal, freezing wind blew mercilessly through the train. As the hour passed, my curiosity quickened.

I had promised myself that I would not think about Don's drinking, but again, fear welled up within me. It was a fear similar to seeing the Black Forest and knowing it sheltered beastly dwellings. Thoughts of alcohol covered my mind like a dark shadow.

At that moment, I realized that Don's drinking truly felt demonic. *It's good to recognize Satan's brew,* I thought to myself. *Be still heart!* I ordered my mind. No, I would not allow fear to manipulate my simple nature. *Dear me, what is happening to my mind?* I wondered. Then my body stopped trembling, and my mind was clearer. "I mustn't allow my faith to weaken," I uttered with brighter hope for the future.

Then after the train had passed beyond the Black Forest, the sound of the train's whistle brought sunlight in. Of course, the sunlight didn't stop my thoughts. I needed to show Don much compassion, for he had promised to give up alcohol. I was convinced that my faithful love would change things if Don failed to keep his promise. After all, Don had put me on a pedestal and would gather the stars for me if possible.

At that moment, my mind focused on the truth. Did Don love me enough to give up alcohol entirely? *God will let me know what I must do,* I convinced myself. "I mustn't be afraid," I uttered softly as I stared out the window.

In another hour, the train was halfway to Furth. In one hour and fifteen minutes, I would arrive at Furth station. I felt exhausted. My body trembled from the cold, so I covered myself with my shawl. I struggled to stay awake but slowly drifted off to sleep.

Suddenly, a large hand was shaking me firmly. The young conductor shouted, "Nixes!" thinking I was German. As the young man yelled into my face, he was trying to tell me that I couldn't stay on the train. What I thought had been a short nap must not have been. The train had stopped. I noticed the man's red mustache, which looked like a red frozen brush. *Red seems to be the hottest place on his face,* I thought to myself.

Why is the conductor upset that I am on the train? Did the agent make a mistake on my ticket? Did the train hit something? Perhaps it's a robbery. What in the world is happening?

Nervously I rose. "What's the matter?" I asked, looking straight into the conductor's large blue eyes. "This is the train going to Furth, correct?" I asked. I then realized that the train was empty. All the passengers had left.

The tall conductor ignored all of my questions. "Come!" he instructed straight and strong and pointed toward a small station. My stomach cramped, but I pulled myself together. I followed the conductor to the small station. He could not explain in English what had happened, so he led me to a young girl inside the station.

The young girl explained, "The conductor failed to check your compartment. He thought that you were a regular on the train and that you knew when to change trains. The train you were on was disconnected, so you were left asleep in the car. The train you were to take is on its way to Furth now. Don't worry. We'll give you a new ticket, for it's our mistake."

In that moment, it all came together. I was wearing the German hat and scarf that Don had sent me. My heart began to flutter like a hummingbird's heart. I dared not let shame turn into self-pity. Truly, my heart wanted to tell the conductor that it was his responsibility to check tickets and that because I looked like a German; he had failed to assist me.

I sat inside the small interchange station. I contemplated why God was testing my patience beyond measure. My tired eyes widened as I groaned. "God, I'm out of patience!" I uttered plaintively and then bit my lip in my burst of anger. Truthfully, I didn't feel that God expected me to have calm endurance. Then my mind raced ahead as it sensed I should not be a foolish young woman. *I must learn perseverance in all circumstances of life,* I reminded myself.

Suddenly, the young girl approached me again. "I'm so sorry. I forgot to remind you that the train to Furth will arrive in two hours." Then the fräulein added sharply, "If it's on time." I was satisfied in that moment. I would be on my way to Furth in two hours. My heart beat joyfully as I thought of being with Don.

Consciously, I had another breathless moment. *Oh, my soul. What will Don think now?* I wondered. While waiting for my arrival to Germany, Don had bitten his fingernails until they looked terrible. Now, I had missed the train to Furth. Unfortunately, I would not arrive at the station by the time we had thought I would. My stomach tightened into knots. My cheeks flushed anxiously as I waited for the next train to Furth.

With temperatures well below freezing, the journey seemed longer. The gusting winds were almost unbearable outside. Often, I felt like I was going to burst into tears, but inwardly, a flow of certainty jolted my consciousness. I could not explain the feeling. I had an overwhelming desire to be nearer to God. *Is He preparing bridges that I must cross?* I contemplated and then prayed that I was wrong.

It was 9:20 p.m. when the train finally arrived at the small station in Furth, Germany. The station was empty. Only a lone taxi waited outside. I spotted Don as he stepped from the taxicab. He wore no coat as usual. *He is such a handsome husband*, I thought.

Don paused a moment as though wiping his eyes and then ran toward me with outstretched arms. "What in the world happened?" Don asked while shaking his head.

After Don let go of me, I steadied myself before answering, "Let's be thankful I'm here," I replied. "Oh, thank God," I said, whispering beneath my breath.

"Well," Don replied uneasily, "I've been waiting three hours for the train." He grabbed his coat from inside the taxi and quickly put it on.

I kept my voice calm and replied sweetly, "Honey, traveling cross-country on a train is exhausting. Yes, I'm late, but my heart is full of love. Sweetheart, it's a very long story," I said with a giggle and then inhaled deeply.

The only conversation inside the taxi was silence and us holding each other closely. Suddenly, Don glanced at me and was annoyed that I had not explained my late arrival. "I deserve to know what happened on the train," he insisted, sitting on the edge of his seat.

I changed the subject quickly when Don asked again. I refused to answer while he used that sharp tone. Sometimes, Don spoke in the same manner when he had been drinking. I pretended not to hear him and replied, "Honey, I can hardly wait to see our new apartment in Furth." That got Don's attention.

Quickly, he expressed his feelings about house hunting. "I know you like lots of room. The house is very large for only the two of us. It was difficult to find a house in Furth to rent," he informed me as his smile dripped with pride.

I looked gratefully at Don. "You worry too much. I'll love the house," I assured him and then gave him a kiss.

I noticed that Don's hazel eyes gleamed as he expressed his love. "Love, we're together again. Dear God, how I love you. You're the most important thing in the world to me," he whispered as he held me tightly.

I wanted Don to hold me forever. *Thank God. Things will be okay*, I told myself with certainty filling my heart.

Because we were riding on streets with icy snow and in a taxi with a hasty driver, it was a savage trip to the small village of Furth. Together, the two of us swayed side to side as we traveled the narrow road with corkscrew turns. I squeezed Don's arm tightly to steady myself. It was an exhilarating ride.

Nervously, Don looked into the mirror and motioned for the driver to slow down. "Drive slowly, sir. I must be certain of the house. Oh, halt!" Don said excitedly.

The long path to the front door welcomed us as gusts of wind stirred branches of dead ivy. I imagined that the birth of new ivy would be apparent come spring's glory.

Once inside the house, I glanced all around. The old house was incredibly clean. Every corner had been touched by Don's thoughtful hands. Only a few large items occupied one of the huge rooms we would be living in. A tall antique dressing mirror with its ancient frame waited to be admired. A small table hugging two chairs and a huge stove decorated the middle of the room. A dozen sweet-scented red roses sat on the window ledge that framed Furth's main street. On each window, there was a spotlessly clean pair of light-gray shutters. The ceiling was extremely high but appeared very clean.

Getting my attention, Don pointed at the stove. Its big belly and tall curved legs guarded three kerosene cans like a knight guarding a palace. As Don filled the stove for the night, he commented as if instructing a young recruit, "Honey, see these kerosene cans? They must be filled every three days." Don continued to talk after swallowing hard from the fumes. "Oh, come see the kitchen," he said proudly, leading the way.

I followed him and was too stunned to think clearly. "Oh, it's huge like the farm kitchen," I said and then giggled. My eyes blinked a few times at the old green stove with its tall legs spreading out like an octopus. On the kitchen wall, flowery green wallpaper perfectly matched the stove's color. The kitchen felt icy cold. "This is really something," I commented honestly. Perhaps those who lived here before us were Irish and not German," I said with a tiny chuckle. Green was everywhere I looked in the kitchen.

My eyes focused on a new black teapot. "I like it," I said to Don and then gave him a wink. I noticed the green cupboard, which had possibly been cracked since the war. "Oh, these poor things have never been painted," I said loudly.

Don had filled the refrigerator with all kinds of goodies, and even though more snow had been predicted, we would have plenty of snacks. As we walked down the long hallway to the big room we would be living in, he surprised me again. "I bought a juicy steak for dinner. I'm hungry. What about you, love?" Don had lovingly and thoughtfully prepared dinner ahead of time, as always, including a bottle of wine.

Don poured me a glass of wine and asked, "Love, why don't you have a glass?"

I looked at him seriously. "Sweetheart, you know I love the taste of wine, but it will make me sick."

Don must have sensed my uneasiness, about his drinking and replied, "Don't worry; I'm too busy to drink in Germany. Afterall, we must celebrate tonight. God knows we've been apart for nearly a year."

"Indeed, my trip convinced me that the army should make changes regarding orders and the transportation of dependents," I shared with Don as he poured another glass of wine. Don drank very little, and I was happy about that.

"Love, don't worry about a thing. I can quit drinking anytime. I'll always take care of you. I just want you to be happy. You're my world," Don said as he embraced me.

We were in love. It was a celebration. If Don wanted a glass of wine, he could have one. In a quiet corner of my heart, I felt it best not to ask too many questions, such as, "Honey, are you drinking alcohol once in a while?" Are you drinking every day?"

My heart couldn't help but think of my loving brother Ken, who would die in the future from alcoholism. Ken often told me and my family those very words. "Sis, please don't worry. I can quit drinking anytime." Now I was hearing those same words from Don, and my heart was beating like a drum.

The next day, Don arranged for three days off from the clinic. I glanced at the corner of the room, and my thoughts burst with excitement. "Honey, it will be fun decorating this big house. This house needs curtains and a few washable rugs," I informed Don and then waited for his comments.

Don grinned in the big mirror and then glanced at me before saying a word. "There's no need for you to fix up the house. Don't worry, love, we'll be moving to post housing," he replied. "Post housing has large rooms, so don't worry about space. You'll also have a maid's quarters. It's completely furnished with everything we'll need. About three miles from the house, there is post shopping for military families," Don explained with wide eyes.

My heart jumped. "How long will that take?" I asked excitedly because of the good news.

"I'm hoping just a few months," said Don, trying to ignore the kerosene fumes.

That afternoon, Don handed me a driver's manual. "Love, I know you'll want to drive as soon as the car arrives at the port. Here's a manual for you. Germany is a dangerous place to drive. People drive very fast, so study the rules well."

That night during dinner, Don dropped his head before explaining something to me. I felt that he wanted to say something else. "Sweetheart, I hate to tell you this since you have only been here a week. The first of February, I am going with my troop for two weeks of training. Oh, how I hate leaving you so soon," he expressed pitifully.

I looked Don in the face with confidence. "I'll be just fine. I'm going to look for a church," I replied.

Don's words cut my heart like a knife. "There are no American churches in Furth or Nuremberg," Don informed me. "The small chapel on base is for soldiers. Dependents aren't permitted to attend it," he said. Our eyes met in a long look. Don's words reminded me that things changed quickly in life. "Love, I don't think you'll find a church. I've decided not to attend church in the future," he said as his face flushed with excitement.

There was a tense silence in the room. "Honey, what has changed you? You once loved going to church with me," I said firmly.

Don was silent and refused to comment. At that moment, it was apparent that Don's lifestyle was different now. He need not explain what my heart had already revealed. *Satan and his demons rejoiced that Don no longer would be going to church,* I thought painfully. It was spiritually clear to me. Don knew that if he attended church, God would convict him of drinking. I felt Don knew this without a doubt, and I was sure of my feelings.

I must not be angry with Don, I told myself. Being angry over his decision not to attend church wouldn't be the Christian way. Don's spiritual life was in bondage. He had chosen a lifestyle that would threaten the future of our marriage. I thought about how Don was so dedicated to his career and had a brilliant mind but now was feeling nonchalant about his walk with God. I feared that Don would have great consequences to face in years to come without God's guidance.

However, I calmed myself. A few minutes later, words came through my spirit. *You married Don in sickness and in health.* Yes, such words were much too valuable to squander. I would preserve the unity of our marriage at all costs. I knew that it would not be an easy journey. *The Bible says that God hates divorce,* I thought, trying to hide my sparks of anxiety.

Before Don and I climbed under our downy blanket, I noticed that his crew cut had grown. A tiny black wave was high in the middle of his head. With rapid adjustments, I warmed myself in his arms. Minutes later, I was snuggled closer to the warmth of his body and satisfied in the moment.

CHAPTER 5

TWO WEEKS HAD passed, and it seemed as though I had lived in one room for years. February would arrive in a few days. I opened my eyes to another unbearable day of freezing weather. Don had left for his post at Furth but had filled the stove with enough fuel for that day. As I opened the huge shutters, sunlight fully embellished the room. The snow was falling. It would be a good day to write my letters to Joan and Mama.

Like a bird with a broken wing, I slowly made my way into the kitchen and grabbed my new teapot. I filled it with water and put it on the stove. Soon it whistled, notifying me that it was ready. With a cup of hot tea, I returned to the warmth of the big room. I straightened my down blanket and crawled beneath it. Day after day, I spent time beneath the blanket just to keep warm. Although the stove was large, it was not sufficient enough to heat the entire house.

While sipping tea, I wrote my letters. My fingers tightened from the cold, which made it almost impossible to write clearly. Minutes later, I read my Bible, which gave me a feeling of hope and renewal. "Count your blessings," I said loudly. "Be content," I assured myself. "Everything will be okay. Through faith, I can do all things."

It was February, and Don was preparing to leave for training on the following Saturday. He would be away two weeks, and my new world was about to open widely. I knew nothing about Furth or Nuremberg, but I realized Germany was very different from the good old USA. I realized the German people were not as friendly as I had expected them to be. Seemingly, German women had no desire to be friends with army wives. I had been warned to be prepared, but I was not.

Unfortuanetly, our supplies, household items, television, radio, and car had not arrived yet. I was ready to smile and to talk to anyone I encountered who had a friendly face. I had not expected a life of seclusion, but Don had warned me that army life would be different from a civilian lifestyle.

During lonely days of solitude, I talked to God almost constantly. I wondered why I felt so much confusion. Was Don drinking because he knew I was barren? I was trying to find answers as to why he was drinking and strangely was blaming myself at the same time. I could do nothing to stop Don's desire for alcohol and did not deny that fact.

When we had lived in Colorado Springs, I had thought I could win the battle against alcohol. Now the devil's brew was mocking me again. I had never thought Don's addiction was as bad as it was, but now I had to accept the truth.

I recalled that before Don left for training, he had given me instructions. I was to make sure that the kerosene cans didn't run out and to study my driver's manual. I hoped that Don would be home on the weekend as he had promised.

The next morning, the temperature hardened the ground like a frozen river. Zero-degree weather deadened the little village of Furth, which stood against the bright blue sky. Like a groundhog pushing its way into the light, I shouted daringly in the large mirror, "Yes, Mama, I'm taking a leap of faith today! I'm going to find myself a church. Surely there's a church somewhere in Furth."

I deeply thought about how blessed I was for having such a strong heritage. I thought about Papa's great-great-grandparents, who settled in Boone, North Carolina, on a plantation that helped to build a church in the early 1800s. I felt grateful that my Christian heritage was so amazing just when I needed it. I felt the need to hurry along triumphantly and follow the path of faith before me. I would find a church where I could worship and always listen for God's whispers in my spirit. Mama's words were with me, "Hold onto your faith."

I took in a long deep breath. "Yes, Mama, I miss home today," I uttered as I searched through unpacked boxes in the corner. Instantly, I spotted my long johns and then put them on. Indeed, I would need thermal underwear that day. Without my long johns, it would be impossible to survive outside with the temperatures well below zero.

As the rebellious wind raged through the morning, I told myself many times how crazy it would be to challenge such freezing weather. I imagined I was losing my mind from solitude. I was like a steamship that was ready to move along with unyielding purpose. This day, I would search for a church and not return until my mission was accomplished.

"Oh, Lord Jesus, rid me of my feelings of uncertainty," I prayed. Of course, it was the uncertainty of Don's drinking that was on my mind constantly. But this day, I would forget about Don's problem and concentrate on my spiritual mission to find a church.

Quick as a falling apple, I put on my leopard-print German hat with matching scarf—the same hat and scarf that the conductor had assumed I was German in. I glanced in the mirror with flushing delight. "Oh my, I do look German all the way," I said loudly, dancing around the room.

In the tall mirror, I smiled confidently, but deep inside, I trembled a little. "God's little frightened lamb in a new world," I blabbered and then bent to turn off the old stove's valve.

Once outside, I was stunned at the sight before me. Everywhere I glanced, Furth appeared to be frozen in ice. It gave off a beautiful silvery glow. The bright sunlight cast shadowy images on the windows of the small shops along my route, but it appeared no one was inside. I walked, shivered with every step, and slipped on the icy sidewalk now and then.

I stopped a moment to adjust my hat, raising it off my nose. How could my head be so cold with such a warm hat? "Oh, goose feathers," I shouted. "Good grief, I'm frozen. I must go back right now," I confessed again and again. My body told me to go home, but determination urged me onward in pursuit of my goal.

For a brief moment, I imagined that the town knew I was a stranger. I felt concerned. Not a soul was outside. Every shop was closed, but I gave this no thought because Germans often closed their shops when notified to do so. "The glorious lamp of heaven is with me today," I gasped, referring to the beam of sunlight slightly warming my face.

Ahead, an adorably quaint shop caught my attention, but I was not sure it was open. I approached the window to see inside it. I breathed on the snowy glass and cleared a small circle with my stiff gloved hand. With wonder, I peered inside. *What harm will it do?* I thought as

CAROLYN L. KEETON

curiosity overcame my good judgment. Slowly I started to walk away, but my nose stuck to the icy window. Dear Lord, had I lost my nose? With an almost unbearable pain, I slowly pulled my nose off the frozen window.

From inside, I heard a sharp voice. "Come in! Come in!" a middle-aged lady shouted. I could not speak German, but the lady spoke some English.

Quickly, I stepped inside the small shop and closed the door to preserve the precious heat. "Thank you!" I said gratefully while taking off my icy gloves.

With a strange look, the lady stared at me for a moment before speaking. "What are you doing out in this freezing weather?" she asked in broken English. "Haven't you heard the news? Today we are informed everyone must remain inside." Suddenly, the German lady checked the door again to make certain I had closed it tightly.

I took a few seconds to collect myself before answering. "I'm hoping to find an American church in Furth. Do you know of one?" I asked as I searched for chocolates.

The German lady spoke again. "I've been told a minister is coming from America to establish a church for the military personnel who are stationed in Furth. There's a rumor a church will be established very soon. I was informed that it would be behind the old Furth wall," the lady added in a secretive manner.

"Where's the old wall?" I asked, hoping my prayers were being answered.

The lady answered as though the war had haunted her deeply. "The old wall hasn't been restored since World War II. Such a dreadful place! Just some old buildings that were not restored after the Nuremberg bombings. I will write down how to get there. Do be careful," she warned, reaching for a notepad.

"Will I be safe behind the old wall?" I asked as I sat down.

The lady's words sounded forced as she put the directions in my hand. "You'll be safe behind the wall, but please don't go there alone." Suddenly the lady changed the subject. "It would be nice to have you visit again," the lady said with gentle kindness in her voice.

I sighed in relief and stuffed the note quickly into my pocket. Before leaving, I pulled out eleven marks to pay for dark chocolates.

Seconds later, I paused at the door. "When I find a job, I shall return to buy that beautiful white china," I promised the lady reassuringly.

The lady spoke loudly and asks, "Would you like me to hold the china for you?"

"That's very nice of you, but I must find a job first," I replied. *I shall come back someday to buy that china,* I told myself. A year later, I returned to the shop to buy my beautiful white Rosenthal china.

As I made my way home, I felt the day had been worth every frozen part of me. I had decided to walk the path of faith as my great-great-grandparents had. I had discovered a church was coming to Furth soon. "Dear Lord, thanks for leading my footsteps. Thanks for leading me to the German lady," I murmured, feeling extremely exuberant.

By midweek, I noticed that the kerosene cans were almost empty. I hurried into the kitchen and counted out thirty marks from a large cookie can. I had to walk half a block to phone for a taxi. Returning home, I sat waiting beside three cans for the taxicab to arrive.

Suddenly a thought flooded my mind. I could vanish from the face of the earth. After all, who knew I existed but my family? Inside the taxi, another fearful thought entered my mind. I was in a foreign country with no protection. The German police authorities were not permitted to assist or to interfere with the army and their dependents stationed in Furth. I wondered who would search for me if I disappeared.

In the taxi, I kept silent for a few minutes and then leaned forward to ask, "Do you speak English?"

The young driver did not reply immediately. After a few seconds, he said, "A little." The man's voice softened. "Is your husband with the army?"

"Yes!" I expressed with a nod while trying not to reveal too much information.

Upon arriving at the kerosene pump half an hour later, the driver offered to fill the cans for me. He struggled with the cans and then quickly loaded them into the taxi. About twenty minutes later, the taxi

CAROLYN L. KEETON

was back in Furth. The man carried the cans to the front entrance with straightforward kindness.

As I filled the stove for the night, I shivered terribly from the unheated room. I was now seeing into a different world where survival was often difficult. My thoughts went up to heaven. "Thank You, God, for living in foreign lands. Please stay close beside me," I whispered prayerfully.

A sudden streak of moonlight came through the window's shutters and lingered there. I felt it was a sign of God's heavenly tenderness. As a young, new bride, I was learning never to start arguments with Don over his drinking thinking he would give up alcohol.

I also considered if Don was ever abusive, divorce would be permissible in the eyes of God. Don had been drinking almost every night after duty hours at the club. Not once had he ever been aggressive toward me. He always ate, showered, and quietly went to sleep.

Don could be immature and even irrational if I mentioned his drinking. No, I dare not bury my head in the sand. I knew well that I was not alone in my struggles. I felt God's amazing grace and loving mercy constantly guiding me.

Outwardly, I smiled, but inwardly, my heart also wept for Don's spiritual life. I could not explain my feelings. I knew that self-examination was a vital part of living a true Christian life. While Don was away, I realized that denial brought a sense of unreality. I prayed for the knowledge to understand Don's addiction, yet feelings of anger often overtook me. I cried out to God furiously, as His Word rested within my spirit. I gained new strength in my daily struggles, although Don's addiction became a compulsive need.

My doubts slowly turned to faith as I wept and prayed in the realization that the Lord Jesus was interceding for me. With this hope, I felt the Holy Spirit would lead me into all truth. Indeed, I had to learn to guard my mind. I knew I would fail now and then. Life's struggles with an addicted spouse were like no others.

Two weeks had passed, and Don's two-week training was over. He arrived from Wurzburg on Saturday at noon. "Love, I couldn't stay away one more day," he whispered softly to me.

"I missed you too," I said with excitement. I immediately got Don's attention when I happily said, "I know all my driving rules. I am ready to take my driver's exam."

Don looked somewhat surprised. "That's great, honey. Perhaps the car will arrive next week. Thank God, we will need no more taxis."

Don took off his combat boots and glanced thoughtfully at me. "Love, Tuesday is the best day to take your driver's exam," he said persuasively. "Tomorrow, I must catch up at the medical clinic. Then Tuesday, I'll take the day off and go with you." Drawing me into his arms, Don said softly, "But right now, I want to hold you forever."

When Tuesday arrived, my heart skipped a few beats. Fortunately, I passed the driver's exam with flying colors. Now I would be able to drive more and tour the country villages when spring arrived. My richest blessing would be locating the new church that was coming to Furth. I tied that thought with a yellow ribbon. I knew that springtime would bring a vastness of beauty.

Valentine's Day brought a blessing. Don came into the house carrying a dozen roses. "Sweetheart, I have good news. The car has arrived. We can pick it up at the port," he shouted as he lifted me into the air.

The next day at noon, Don and I took a taxi to pick up the car at the port near Nuremberg. That night, I ventured to ask a question that I knew better than to ask him. In doing so, I failed to keep my promise never to mention the word *alcohol* to Don. "Honey, how can you love me and drink every night but not on Sundays?"

Don tossed me a look of extraordinary pity. "I am not hurting you," he commented from his state of denial.

"How can you say that?" I demanded. "It's because of your drinking that our lives are changing quickly," I remarked abruptly and then reminded myself not to say another word.

Don clenched his teeth before answering. "Now you behave, little squaw," he commented as he reached for my hand.

The next morning while driving Don to his post, I said to him, "Do you think your drinking is pleasing to God?"

Don sighed in a worrisome way. "Honey, I'll deal with my problem. Let's leave God out of this. Please don't worry about my drinking. I am in control," he expressed.

Suddenly, Don raised his voice in apprehension. "Good Lord, look out there. You're driving on the wrong side of the road. You caused an old man who was riding his bike to go into that field. Poor soul! Don't forget. You're not driving stateside," Don remarked and then gave a deflated sigh.

When we arrived, there was a brief good-bye kiss. "Are you going to the club after duty?" I asked, hoping Don would say no.

He looked deeply into my eyes without saying anything. I knew by the look on his face that he would be drinking with his buddies at the club. It was at that moment when I truly understood that I would never be able to discuss Don's drinking in a peaceful conversation.

I wondered how in the world Don drank so much, and always faithful to his job. He was always on time for duty, seldom appeared to be hung over, and always paid all the bills on time. How could that be? Was God still watching over Don?

Indeed, Don was in denial about his addiction. I had learned by being around alcoholics my whole life. His denial was part of him. Some alcoholics admit that they are alcoholics. Alcoholics who live in self-denial have a strong mental power that is beyond belief. Alcoholics who are in self-denial and die because of their alcoholism never confess they are addicted to alcohol.

I prayed continually, yet Satan still attacked my mind. I knew that I could do nothing to help Don's addiction but pray. In my distress, a thought entered my mind. Perhaps if I locked Don in his room, he might sweat out his alcohol and return to the normal being that I had once known. I realized that being a born-again Christian who had been baptized in the Holy Spirit did not stop my irrational thinking. I also felt that Satan was putting thoughts in my mind along with fear.

Night after night, the smell of alcohol lingered on Don's breath. Spending late hours out with his buddies at clubs and beer gardens seemed to be a comfortable lifestyle for him. Though I had plenty to eat, pretty clothing, and money to spend, I felt as though Don wasn't concerned that our marriage was in disarray. His craving for alcohol appeared to be all that mattered.

"What is so upsetting about a husband having a few drinks?" Don asked impulsively one evening. I felt like a rocket ready for flight, and I was emotionally drained. I gave Don no reply.

The monster of alcohol had released its devious power. The positive attitude that I had once had was beginning to slip away. Don's lifestyle, during this time, was crippling my life spiritually. It was becoming difficult to guard my mind and to keep thinking reassuring thoughts daily.

Before long, the Holy Spirit inspired my heart. I realized that I dare not let my positive outlook on life slip away. My faith had to be firm so that I could overcome what lay ahead. God had brought me into His light. However, just thinking about Don's alcoholism gave my heart tremendous pain.

Yes, it was often difficult to face the truth, but I knew that God demanded *truth*. When we live for Jesus Christ, we must also dedicate our lives to him in *truth*. "The LORD *is* near to all who call upon Him, to all who call upon Him in truth" (Ps. 145:18 NKJV).

I believed that Satan was determined to rule Don's life through addiction. Only God could bring Don back to his spiritual life and to serving Him as he once had.

Our beautiful times—planning, praying, hoping, and walking together—were slipping away. It was during this time that I thought about the inevitable subject of love. God already knew that my heart was losing love. Don and I were like ships passing silently by each other in the night. Either he or I was always saying, "I am sorry." Somehow, our love had drifted behind a dark cloud without a silver lining.

I never doubted that God would fill my heart with love once again. Of course God would. *God is love!* I reminded myself daily.

I knew Don's drinking had filled my heart with bitterness. The words of the psalmist cautioned me to examine my heart: "Examine me, O LORD, and prove me; Try my mind and my heart" (Ps. 26:2 NKJV).

Somehow, I had convinced myself that I had every right to have a hardened heart and to believe that Don would realize he was destroying our love. Still, I trusted the faithfulness of God: "Let us hold fast the confession of *our* hope without wavering, for He who promised *is* faithful" (Heb. 10:23 NKJV).

I imagined my painful heart to be like the seasons. When Don and I met, love was like springtime in all of its glory. Then alcohol entered our lives, and love became like a winter's wrath in the Black Forest.

Prayer opened my heart so that God could be my confident companion. I had known since I was a young girl of twelve that His infinite love was like no other. I had also learned in my Bible that kindness and sympathy were great gifts from God. I would remember those words. I would remind myself not to show bitterness and to keep my patience when Don was drinking.

In the months that followed, my positive attitude returned as I prayed for God's perfect will. I believed that was the way to live the Christian life. I already knew that we must all give our struggles daily to God for our well-being. I was inspired to believe that *acceptable* means being worthy and accepted in the eyes of God. I knew that He would accept my struggles and help me.

Continually, I confessed my sinful thoughts to the Lord in prayer. Often, I felt as though all the demons had come from hell to torment my mind. I could not ignore such feelings, which often took away my peacefulness.

"The best is yet to come," I told myself while lying in the morning light. "Satan, you may shadow my peace at times, but I'll win in the end," I shouted out daily to the devil.

In March, a window unbelievably opened into another world that I had never known existed in military life. It was a world of neglected wives and adulterous acts—mostly caused by alcohol addiction.

Deep within my heart, I knew that Don would never physically harm me. I accepted this as a blessing and felt the grace of God watching over me.

In early March 1964, I awoke vigorously at dawn for a very good reason. Easter would arrive in a few weeks and good things were about to happen. The German lady at the little shop had given me the right information. An American minister had arrived in Furth to establish a church behind the old Furth wall.

On Easter Sunday, Don was sleeping soundly. I left a note and slipped quietly out. When the time was right, I would tell Don that a church was now in Furth.

I gave myself half an hour more than usuals so that I could locate the church before it started. Excitement filled me from my head to my toes as I turned the key in the ignition of the car. I rolled the window down, as the birds chirped on the streets and from the tops of buildings to welcome spring's birth. I felt spring unfolding and imagined God's little creatures were singing for my victory of finding out about the church.

While driving to the church, I was deep in thought. I felt that every dewdrop that twinkled in the morning sun gave a conscious praise to God. The waves on the mighty oceans sent alluring songs in the wind, and the sunrise falling on sweet meadows praised Him.

As I drove slowly behind the old Furth wall, it did not take long to see that muddy fields were drenched by spring's rain. Most buildings that had been bombed during the war still stood. However, most of them were in a fallen-down state.

"This place feels creepy," I uttered as I maneuvered the wheel of the car. The car slid terribly in the mud, but I drove onward. "Where's the church?" I murmured again, looking all around the field. Then I had to stop on the narrow road because it seemed that it was impossible to go any further.

Ahead, the narrow road, which was half dirt and half concrete, was broken in pieces. Huge chunks of concrete were lying everywhere. I whispered, "Lord, I shouldn't be here alone." Deciding to walk, I parked the car. *Surely the church must be nearby*, I assured myself while walking onward.

Another field appeared from behind a huge building. Right away, I noticed that cars were parked tightly together. "Where's the church?" I uttered again, trembling from April's chill. From across the field, I heard voices singing loudly, "When we all get to heaven."

"Ah, that's it," I uttered as flocks of birds flew from the field. How wonderful it felt to hear people singing in English. I sucked in a deep breath as my feet sunk into the muddy field. "The Lord will have to rapture these poor souls to get them out of this mud. Oh, how dumb of me not to wear my boots," I grumbled over and over to myself. My feet felt frozen from the mud.

Then I thought of something else. Don would be angry if I got stuck in this forsaken place. What would I tell him if that were to happen?

Minutes later, I saw a rusty old building that was three stories high and approached it. The sunlight shone upon the building as if streaks of silver and reddish rust dripped from it. I noticed that decay had accumulated terribly on its war-torn framework.

Quickly, I entered through the rusty, silver-colored door and then climbed about thirty steps. I paused for a moment at the top. I listened at the door and could hear people jumping all around the room, shouting, and singing. *What's going on?* I thought nervously. "Oh Lord, this must be a Pentecostal church," I uttered. "Lord, why would you lead me to a Pentecostal church? You know I am a Baptist," I whispered. There is no way that I could have known that as years went by, my faith would become Pentecostal.

Cautiously, I stepped inside. Within seconds, a tall gentleman greeted me. "Welcome! Welcome!" he shouted as he ran toward the door to be sure I had closed it tightly.

Then another man explained, "No, we're not Pentecostal. This is a good old Baptist church. We all dance to keep warm. There's no heat in the building, but we dance before the Lord," he yelled to me while jumping back and forth.

From a large loft that was four feet above us, Pastor Green began speaking. "I imagine this old building weeps for the souls of those who lived in the past. It was used during the Nuremberg War to transport war prisoners to the Palace of Justice at Nuremberg for trial. We know there's no heat, but God sees the situation."

Pastor Green trembled as he preached from the Holy Bible, and then he danced a little bit in between. His deep-sounding voice echoed loudly. The pastor wanted to be sure that we heard the good gospel.

The old building vibrated as we all danced. Standing six feet six inches, his legs were as long as Abraham Lincoln's legs. They displayed this faithful servant.

The next week, the pastor's prayer was answered when the army heard his need and delivered a huge heater. Unfortunately, it failed to heat the airy building, so people continued to dance happily and to lose much weight on Sundays.

The following Sunday, I met Sara, who was a tall blond girl. Sara was kind, soft-spoken, and very slim with long graceful legs. Unfortuantely, Sara's eye wandered to the right because of a birth defect. Sara's voice echoed as she spoke through the noise. "I am so happy you came back to church. My husband, Tom, is from Tulsa, Oklahoma. We've been stationed in Germany more than a year. I am a Georgia peach," Sara said and then laughed. "This is my little Lisa. She's three," she commented eloquently.

I felt as though I had known Sara a lifetime. Month after month, the two of us danced with Lisa while holding hands. Sara's husband, Tom, was somewhat like Don's spiritual walk.

"Tom no longer desires to attend church. He is drinking too much," Sara expressed, revealing how much grief was in her heart.

One Sunday after church, Sara mentioned her job. "There's an opening in the accounting department. Carolyn, why don't you apply at the Palace of Justice for an interview? Major Joe is very nice to work for. You'll like him a lot," Sara suggested as she gave me a thin-lipped smile.

"The Palace of Justice employs Americans for office work. The United States has contracts with Germany at corporate headquarters. Most of the work is in data entry on the first floor," Sara said, with encouragement.

"Thanks, Sara," I replied, feeling so grateful to have met her.

Sara's eyes turned bright blue before she remarked, "Let's try to enjoy life before getting too old." Then Sara commented alarmingly, "Besides, Tom is home very little lately. I have seen alcohol destroy many marriages." I was somewhat surprised that Sara had shared her feelings about her husband's drinking too much German beer.

As I said good-bye to Lisa, I gave her a kiss on the cheek. I longed deeply for a baby of my own. When I returned home to post housing, Don was still sleeping off his nightly drinking. Later, he was happy that I had found a church. He never failed to ask me to pray for him.

When Monday arrived, I was filled with enthusiasm. I entered the Palace of Justice and then paused in the huge entrance hall. As I looked up, I noticed large steel loops hanging from the ceiling. "Those steel loops held prisoners who were sentenced to be hung during the war trials," the guardsman said informatively.

My throat tightened. "Oh, gee," I replied and then quickly walked toward the steps. My heart pounded rapidly as I climbed what appeared to be a tower of steps. I walked down the palace's long hallway and located Major Joe's office immediately.

"Hello, major. Shall I come in or wait in the hall? Oh, by the way, I'm Sara's friend Carolyn," I said enthusiastically.

"Certainly, come in," the major replied cheerfully. "I've been expecting you. Sara told me last week that you would be coming for an interview. This place is like home, so just relax. You will start in data entry, and then I'll get you transferred here with me and Sara in accounting," he informed me.

The major's dark-gray suit gave me the impression that it had been tailored. He informed me later that he had to renew his United States' citizenship because he had fallen in love with his German wife Ingrid during the war. Major Joe was not required to wear a U.S. airforce uniform, but I often saw him wearing one. He was employed with the German and US governments. I noticed that the major's gold watch flashed brilliantly against his copper-like suntan.

I looked eagerly out the window. I could not resist enjoying the scenery whenever I was near a window—a habit I could not seem to break. The major walked toward the window and then explained, "What you see below is a place where prisoners once walked. Day after day, prisoners walked that narrow cobblestoned courtyard as they awaited trial." Then the major retorted, "Oh, what a bloody war!" and then breathed a sigh of relief. I noticed that when the major mentioned the war, his eyes filled with tears.

I listened carefully as the major continued. "I know you'll like working with Sara and me, even though Americans are paid very little. The hourly wage for Americans is seventy-five cents an hour," the major informed me as his dark eyes gleamed.

Major Joe was a true mentor. He was very knowledgeable and had an extraordinary personality. His black eyes twinkled with every word. I deeply sensed in my spirit that the major loved people of all races. Indeed, I was thankful for the seventy-five-cent hourly wage.

It had been a stressful interview, but I had maintained my composure. "Thank you, major. I'll see you Monday morning," I assured Major Joe.

I felt marvelous. Excitement took control of me. I could hardly wait to tell Don about my job. For the very first time, I felt that God had intervened in my life. I could move on with hope and perhaps keep my mind off Don's drinking.

I had been feeling that I was becoming Don's nurse. I thought that if Don was drinking too much, I must be home. Often, I feared that when he smoked, he might set the house on fire. Because of my new job, at last, I was thinking of myself.

At around nine o'clock that night, Don arrived home. He was late. I explained about my new job. He cracked his knuckles and then commented, "Love, why would you want to work? Don't you have a nice home? We waited months to move into post housing. You have a maid. Life is good," he complained with concern.

"It was your idea to hire a maid to help once a week because the bathtub is so deep I cannot reach the bottom of it," I replied.

I searched my mind for some way to make Don understand. "Yes, you're doing just fine. You don't understand, do you? Night after night, I'm here alone waiting for your loving return, writing poetry, and cooking. I have no car to drive because you have it. Don, this is 1964, and we don't know when we'll be facing another war. Tom remarked that the United States and North Vietnamese troops have exchanged live fire. Have you been told about troops receiving orders for North Vietnam?" I asked.

CAROLYN L. KEETON

Don replied, "We've been informed that things could change within the year. Soviet aggression is beginning to escalate in proxy wars," he said, changing the subject quickly.

Don made a face. "Well, I see your mind is made up. So be it. Take the job at the palace," he answered resentfully.

In mid-June of 1964, Pastor Green made a disheartening announcement to the fellowship. "My wife, Helen, is seriously ill, and we must leave for Texas. I am so sorry there won't be a church anymore. I have been informed that no pastor will be taking my place. God be with you all at this time," Pastor Green informed us tearfully. Indeed, the church fellowship was in shock. I was as sad as the others that the church would be gone and that fate would be in command once again.

A month later, I decided to attend Saint Lorenz Cathedral in the heart of Nuremberg. "It must be a beautiful cathedral," I said to Sara during work. "Please, let's visit on our lunch hour," I suggested. I noticed that she hesitated before answering.

Sara seemed somewhat surprised. "It's raining outside," she replied as she glanced out the window. Then Sara rubbed her hands together and said, "Today, I must catch up on work." She gave the major a cool glance. "We will visit next Friday," Sara answered.

I reached for my raincoat. Major Joe removed his glasses and then said, "As an airforce pilot, I was ordered to bomb Nuremberg during World War II." Once again, I noticed that he seemed ashamed of the tears that filled his eyes.

The major's eyes widened, and he was silent for a moment before continuing. "Carolyn, why don't you take the day off? You've been working steadily for months. You need a break. I want you to do something special for yourself today, or better yet, why not fly to Copenhagen with the three of us on Saturday? I am flying my own plane there. My wife, Ingrid, and I invited Sara and Lisa to come along for the weekend too. Come join us, and we'll make it a real family vacation. You'll love Copenhagen. Then you can see a real pilot in flight," the major said and then laughed. He was so confident of his flying expertise.

I grinned at the major. "You know that Don would never agree to that," I replied. "However, I would like a day off," I said to the major. I noticed the major's hands were trembling, which was uncharacteristic of him. Often, Don's hands trembled in the same way. This seemed to be the handwriting on the wall. I recognized his problem clearly.

I recalled the major's words from the previous week as the three of us had been having lunch in the palace courtyard. "I'm terribly addicted to alcohol. War does terrible things to a man's mind," the major had commented that afternoon. Often, the smell of the liquor he had drunk the night before lingered on his breath, and his large black eyes were red.

I suppose the devil's demons are shaking the major's life, I thought sorrowfully. I had hoped I was wrong, but I was not. *For pity sake, how I wish countries would pass a law of abstinence,* I thought. My heart had felt as though it would burst inside my chest as I realized Major Joe had confessed he was addicted to alcohol.

Sara never got behind in her work. She was only using it as an excuse not to visit the cathedral that day. Sara wanted to stay behind to encourage the major because he was having a bad day. It was understandable. The major was like a father to both of us. We admired the major's gentle kindness and the good advice he always gave.

At exactly noon, I eagerly made my way to the cathedral. The rain had almost stopped. The lilies were pushing up through the dirt as June rains kissed every bloom. As I walked, my eyes scanned every house. Every window box was filled with lovely flowers. Even the lilies stirred my heart to reflect. *Love between a husband and a wife is often difficult to understand,* I thought as I shoved my umbrella into its pouch.

In the distance, the cathedral was magnificent. Suddenly, a twinkle of sunlight appeared on its highest spires. Two steellike man-made crowns appeared to be a pale faded-green color and were mounted high on each side of the roof. They glistened in the sunlight because they were wet from the rain. This caused them to change many beautiful colors. Then within seconds, the sky was sunless.

Saint Lorenz Cathedral was built in the thirteenth century. Its large rose Romanesque stained-glass windows were a wondrous sight that my eyes had never seen before.

CAROLYN L. KEETON

I felt somewhat strange being a Protestant as I entered the cathedral. After all, in the sixties, Protestants did not attend Catholic churches and vice versa. I could not clearly see the beautifully detailed carvings because of the cloudy day. At first, it all seemed very strange, for I had never been inside a cathedral before, but then a feeling of peace filled my spirit.

A petite lady, whom I had failed to see from the back of the cathedral, rose quickly to leave. After a few minutes, I knelt in front of the altar to pray. I wanted to tell God how disappointed I felt. After all, He had not answered my prayers about Don's drinking. "I have tried to be a good wife, Lord. I'm trying hard to serve you faithfully. Please, Lord, don't forget me," I pleaded.

I had many complaints to bring to God, but I felt He must be tired of hearing my cries. "Lord, I don't know why I came today," I whispered. "Perhaps I came because I miss my church fellowship." After pouring out my complaints to God, I prepared to leave. Just as I started to rise from the altar, warmth covered my body. I felt as though someone had poured warm water over me.

I glanced all around. *Who would do such a thing?* I wondered and then realized that I was alone. I glanced around the cathedral again. Suddenly like a cool breeze, words came through my spirit: *Some day, you'll have children.* My heart felt like it was beating in my ears. "God, is that your voice?" I uttered almost in tears as I wondered what in the world was happening.

Because I did not understand what was taking place in that moment, fear shot down my spine. I shuddered, but then my heart filled with such radiant joy. "Thank You, Lord. I'm not a barren young wife after all. Oh Lord, Don will never believe all this when I tell him," I said too loudly.

At around 2:15 p.m., I left the cathedral. Because I was full of excitement, I decided to shop in the city. Turning a corner, I noticed a baby shop in front of me. "Oh!" I mumbled as I peeked in through the window. There, a small blue hand-knit sweater laid pleading like a tiny puppy to be taken home. *Oh, do I've enough marks to buy it?* I wondered, reaching my hand inside my German shopping bag.

Then I remembered that I had purchased German marks just two days earlier. Quickly, I counted out twenty marks, which were equal to five American dollars. "Great. Just enough for the sweater set," I said, giggled, and then opened the door.

Once inside the small gray shop, I walked toward the sweater set. The German salesgirl spoke no English. I picked up the sweater and walked quickly over to her. I pulled out my marks and let her know that I wanted to buy the sweater set.

I knew how to count out marks, so the young girl knew that I was paying for it. Patiently, the fräulein wrapped and tied it with a white ribbon. Perhaps she thought it was a gift. No indeed, it was for my future baby. The Holy Spirit did not lie. God had spoken to me, and I belived Him.

Within the hour, I returned to the palace headquarters. I breathed a sigh of relief, for my arrival was just in time. The old army transport bus was loaded and ready to take American employees to post housing. "Thank heavens. The bus hasn't left," I mumbled as I quickly jumped on.

I breathed deeply and stopped trembling. Oh how I hated to go home when Don wasn't there. My pulse rose rapidly. I had to go home. *When he gets home, I must tell him about my experience at the cathedral,* I thought, hoping that Don would be home early.

Upon arriving at post housing, I realized how good it felt to be in high spirits. About a half an hour later, I secretly placed the sweater set in the bottom of my dresser drawer. I was so excited that I needed to tell someone about my experience at the cathedral. Quickly, I dialed Sara's number, only to realize that Sara had already left for Copenhagen with the major and his wife, Ingrid.

I cooked dinner and waited patiently for Don's arrival. At 9:30 p.m., I heard the key turn in the lock. Don was home early from the club. As usual, he was happy and laughing from too much liquor.

As Don walked toward the kitchen, he asked, "Honey, what's for dinner?"

"A rich supply of pinto beans, cornbread, and fried potatoes," I said and then added, "While you're eating, I have great news to tell you."

Don's eyes widened as I explained my experience at the cathedral. When I had finished, he commented, "You don't believe that really happened, do you? Good Lord, are you smashed on that malt beer you've been drinking to gain weight?"

"Sweetheart, we both know we will never have a baby of our own, but we can take Captain Smith's advice and go to Italy for an adoption. You just imagined those words at the cathedral. That's right. Please stop punishing yourself. I knew before we got married that you would never be able to have a child," Don remarked with tearful, loving words.

My heart seemed to stop for a moment as I sensed tension in Don's voice. It was a sign that let me know he did not believe me. My greatest disappointment had happened when we had first been married. Don had doubted the doctors and had believed we would have children. His faith had once been steadfast that God would someday grant a miracle. However, now his faith had drifted away. *Its okay*, I told myself. *Who could really believe such an experience happened?*

For several months, Dons'words haunted me endlessly. Not a day went by when my heart did not focus on my religious experience at the cathedral.

When Monday morning arrived, I could hardly wait to tell Sara and the major. After all, they were dear friends, and I had no doubt that they would believe my experience. I entered the room quietly. Major Joe cleared his throat and looked at me strangely. He blinked a few times before he spoke. "Well, I see my good advice worked. Carolyn, you look so rested," he said with a smile.

I answered quickly, "Major, I need to tell you and Sara what happened on my day off. While I was visiting Saint Lorenz Cathedral and praying, a wonderful thing happened." With excitement, I explained everything that had taken place at the cathedral.

The major smiled at me and then blinked again. He looked over at Sara's desk and nodded his head in dismay. "I am worried about you, Carolyn," said Major Joe. "Perhaps Don's drinking is affecting you physically and more than you realize," the major commented with tiny wrinkles of concern on his face.

The major took in a deep breath and then continued, "Of course, a baby in the midst of a crisis isn't a good thing, although I must admit that my four children saved my life. It was my kids that helped me recover after the war," Major Joe said as his eyes sparkled brighter than usual while thinking of his children.

I answered with assuredness. "Major, I think every woman longs to feel the warmth of a baby's love. You should know this. You and Ingrid have four children. Children make us strong and help us to live well," I added with a smile. I felt somewhat sad for the major.

Sara was silent during the conversation but spoke softly after we were finished, "I know how much you love Lisa. She has taken to you as if you were her mother. Perhaps you want a baby so much that you imagined it was God's voice," Sara remarked as she glanced toward the major's desk.

I felt so annoyed at Sara's comment. "Sara, how can you say that? Someday, you'll be sorry you doubted me," I said to her. I realized that no one believed my miracle. I would have to wait for God to fulfill His promise, and that would be just fine. If He took years to do it, I would wait patiently.

The next day, I said to Sara, "It is okay, Sara, that you and Major Joe do not believe my experience," I remarked with disappointment in my voice. Daily, I tenderly caressed the tiny blue sweater set as though a baby already filled it. From that day forward, I never doubted for one moment that the Holy Spirit had whispered within my heart. I considered it pure joy that God had loved me so much to have spoken to my spirit. No indeed, He had not forgotten me.

CAROLYN L. KEETON

CHAPTER 6

IN THE MONTHS that followed, I would cuddle the tiny blue sweater set in my arms and then would place it gently back in the dresser. Don's drinking prompted me to examine my heart. No, I mustn't die each day because of his drinking. At this time, Don's addiction felt like the death of a spouse to me. Once again, my faith was faint. I experienced feelings of anger, depression, denial, and acceptance—the same emotions that occur as when a loved one dies.

God knows our hearts. He desires that we live in a well-balanced way and free from bondage, I reminded myself each day. I also believed that a woman's inner strength was a gift from God and that a husband didn't have any right to intrude upon his wife's inner strength. A woman's inner strength was to be honored by her husband.

Months later, I became wonderful friends with Joan, Pat, and other wives of Don's drinking friends. Joan had decided to leave Jim since he was drinking too much after duty hours. Joan had returned to her parents' home with her and her husband's new baby. Pat and Gary constantly had disputes over his drinking. Therefore, seeing lives torn apart because of alcohol was adding deeper pain to my life. I know that God grieves for *His people* and loves those who are addicted to alcohol but abhorres the sin of it.

By the end of August, Don asked something of me that surprised me. "Love, please come with me to the club. Army wives go to clubs with their husbands. Most wives don't even drink alcohol. Come. We'll dance, and that's all," Don suggested, hoping I would agree with him.

The next weekend, he brought up the subject again, and I decided to go with him. That summer, I decided to go with Don to the club nearly every weekend. I told myself, *Don has a right to ask*. Although after a few months, feelings of conviction lay heavily upon my heart. By the end of the summer, I felt that a fearful separation from God had occurred. I had broken my promise to never let night clubs or alcohol become a lifestyle. I had given in to Don's wishes, and now guiltiness had overcome me. I realized as a true Christian, I shouldn't take part in the devil's world of clubbing. I had made a terrible mistake.

At times, I closed my eyes and tried to remember what it had been like when I had felt God holding my trembling hands. I desired to feel that way again. My heart was in deepest misery, and I did not need any more stress than I already had.

The following Saturday night at the club, an event from the past visited my mind. I remembered a pig contest that had been held at the Ohio Lucasville Fair when I had been a young maiden of thirteen. A fat young pig had been greased from head to toe and then put into a small arena. Later, lionhearted young men would challenge young maidens in this competition. At the end of the contest, judges would decide which team had held the greasy pig the longest.

As I reminisced, seizing the pig that day. I realized, that Satan's world is alcohol and drugs – all found in most nightclubs where unclean spirits influence people's lives.

"Okay, God! You got my attention. No more clubs," I uttered in a shrill voice. "What did you say, love?" Don asked loudly. "Watch Hank play that steel guitar," he said and then laughed. I was quiet and unperturbed at that moment. Don put his arms around me, squeezing me tightly. "Honey, I hate to tell you this. Next Saturday, I must take my medical unit to Berchtesgaden. I'll be away again for at least two weeks," he explained passionately. Even though I was dreadfully sad that Don would be leaving so soon, I accepted the fact that army life meant sudden changes.

At sunrise the next morning, I realized something wonderful. God was taking care of the issue of the club. I felt wholeheartedly that I must make the right decision before Don arrived home for the evening. When Don arrived home, I said, "I am not going to the club anymore. I'm sorry, honey, but my spirit feels condemned with so much chronic drunkenness."

There was no argument, and it was settled quickly. I would not be going with Don to clubs and was prepared for words of betrayal.

CAROLYN L. KEETON

"Well, that's your decision," Don said seriously and then walked toward the kitchen for a beer. "Do you really believe God sends people to hell over going to a club or a few drinks?" he asked.

I calmly replied, "Only our heavenly Father is our judge. Of course, you know that."

I wanted to be liked by the friends I had made, but I had made a choice. I longed to feel close to God as I had once had. I realized this would never happen if I continually walked further away from Him.

The spiritual battle returned again and was frightening. Resentment, arguments, criticism, deceitfulness, and bitterness resided deep within me each day as I prayed faithfully for God to take them away. In prayer, I made every attempt to rid myself of those feelings as Don's drinking became much worse.

On Saturday morning as Don left for Berchtesgaden, I vowed that my face would not show signs of anger. Don's smile broadened as he said good-bye. "You and Sara can visit Berchtesgaden. Tom's unit will also be going. I expect that Tom and I will be home one weekend. When we return, the five of us will tour Rothenburg ob der Tauber. Sweetheart, please prepare the emergency kit like the army requested," Don suggested as he embraced me tightly.

Minutes after Don left, my mind had no rest. Don had just left, but my inmost thoughts still stirred. *Will he be drinking there? What excuses will he give for drinking?* I wondered. My inner compulsions felt like a burning fire that was out of control.

Alone that night, I remembered Lewis Farm and my horse, Star. Star was a very prudent young mare and had good judgment at all times. The one-quarter thoroughbred in her brought out her elegant traits magnificently. Star's black coat was as luminous as the stars. Her long thin legs were swift. Dad had told the family that Star was of good breeding.

I recalled an incident when Star had foreseen danger and had shown fear. I had tried to force Star to jump across a wide creek, but she had refused. Like a streak of lighting, Star had turned suddenly and galloped toward the barn for shelter where she would feel safer and be out of danger.

Minutes later, I breathed a sigh of relief. "Lord, you're my shelter in times like these. Please keep reminding me," I uttered. Star brought to mind that even those of us who have faith are weak, frail, and vulnerable at times.

Star was prudent. I contemplated what *prudent* really meant. I glanced at the unpacked boxes that were stacked in the bedroom closet and then sifted through them. "There's my dictionary!" I shouted. Then I looked up the definition of the word *prudent*: careful to avoid errors, exercising sound judgment, practical wisdom, and discretion; entices knowing or foreseeing. Most certainly, Star had these fine qualities and more.

If God created Star to be so prudent, surely He will do much more for me, my young mind believed. Suddenly a Scripture spoke to my spirit: "House and riches *are* an inheritance from fathers, *but* a prudent wife *is* from the LORD" (Prov. 19:14 NKJV).

"Whoopee! God is revealing that I can become a prudent wife," I mumbled while clasping my hands. *Yes indeed, the Lord is teaching me how to become a wise woman*, I assured myself. In my mind, I was confident that God would teach me within a week.

I had failed to understand that throughout our lives, God teaches us prudence. I considered that wise women made genuine choices in bad situations. I decided to relinquish my will to God, not only on good days but also in extremely bad circumstances. I would be constantly open to God and would have great expectations of what He could do as He displayed the greatness of His power.

I soon recognized that to wait in expectation was a powerful example of bringing burdens before the Lord. My spirit felt like it was humming a little tune and thinking positive thoughts about the future. I believed that embracing positive thoughts would someday make me a prudent wife. I came to the understanding that God instructs us in wisdom so that we may walk in His paths.

I felt Don's addiction had caused me to lose focus on myself. Therefore, it was important to remember that Satan would attempt to stand in the way of my keeping a positive faith.

CAROLYN L. KEETON

The task would not be an easy one. If I expected my prayers to be answered, I must wholeheartedly have forgiveness in my heart toward Don. I knew that God was displeased with my unforgiving heart. I believed, *what other way can I be healed except by forgiveness?*

The Bible taught me that only God gave wisdom in life's struggles. I did not understand Don's lifestyle or how I could help him. Indeed, I saw that the world of addictions was filled with deceitful ways. I could not trust my own feelings in times of crisis. I had to trust in the Holy Spirit to guide me with wisdom, or our marriage would end.

Eventually, I learned that God speaks to us in our struggles through His Word. My self-worth reflected a pity-poor image, and my heart was divided into a million tiny pieces. I trusted the Holy Spirit's guidance as I read the words of the psalmist: "For this *is* God, Our God forever and ever; He will be our guide *even* to death" (Ps. 48:14 NKJV).

The following Saturday morning, Sara and I joined Don and Tom at Berchtesgaden. That afternoon, Tom had to fly a mission in his helicopter and had taken on extra duty. I sensed that Sara felt neglected. Don had also been given an unexpected duty as well at the clinic. Since both men were working long hours, we decided to return to Furth.

"Darn it!" Sara shouted. "Tom lives to fly a helicopter. If it wasn't for Lisa, Tom would divorce me in a minute." Sara sobbed angrily.

I quickly reminded Sara that Tom loved her dearly. Even so, I had never met a woman that did not admire Tom's handsome face, bluest eyes, and pleasant personality. I never doubted that Tom and Don appealed to many fräuleins' hearts. Because they had handsome faces and good natures, German women took notice.

Unfortunately, Don drank alcohol like no other person I had ever known. At times, the pain caused by Don's drinking was unbearable. I irrationally hoped he would get terribly sick from the alcohol. There was no doubt in my mind that after duty, he would head to the club to drink. I never saw Tom high and knew that he would watch Don closely. *How can this be?* I wondered. *Is God watching over Don even when he is drinking heavily?*

Don always seemed happy and content with life and was seldom moody. I felt as though my prayers for Don were keeping him alive and out of trouble.

After returning to Furth on Sunday morning, Sara, Lisa, and I left for the small village of New Market. As we entered the antiquated village, everything was quiet and still. Not a soul was stirring. It was as though everyone had vanished from the town. It gave us a very creepy feeling.

Lisa pointed toward a house. "See, Mommy, Jesus on a cross. Jesus is hanging on that house," Lisa shouted and then gave a little giggle.

"Yes, honey," Sara answered. Then Sara's voice rose with excitement. "Oh, my soul, look at that cross. I have never seen a cross like that. Well, I declare. I'm so impressed by this old village," Sara commented and then sighed.

I glanced at the cross. "Neither have I," I replied. "I imagine everyone is attending mass. No one seems to be outside," I said to Sara as I parked my car.

The three of us strolled down the narrow cobblestoned street for nearly a block. When we came to a small wooden bench, Lisa urged Sara to sit awhile in the morning sunlight.

"I want to find that house with the cross on it—the one we saw when we entered the village. Sara sit awhile with Lisa and walk down later," I insisted.

As I walked down the cobblestoned street for half a block, the cross suddenly glittered like diamonds as sunlight shone directly onto it. A huge cross covered the front of a small white house. "Wow!" I said loudly. "This cross must be as ancient as New Market itself," I uttered, feeling overwhelmed by such an incredible handmade masterpiece.

As I examined the cross's magnificent craftsmanship, I felt the need to pray before the cross. I poured my heart out to God. "Jesus, Don has walked away from you. He is not the same man that I married. I am filled with confusion and disappointment. Don's drinking is dishonorable," I said softly. In that moment, it occurred to me that it was okay to feel anger but that I shouldn't use that anger against others.

As the morning sunlight shone upon the cross, the passionate face of Christ gave me peace and assurance. It was no wonder that thousands toured the small village at New Market just to see such a beautiful old cross. *Someday I shall write a poem about this unbelievable cross*, I thought.

Lisa came running toward me, and then Sara appeared. "What do you think of this cross?" Sara asked.

"God led us here today. Sara, I'm convinced that fate had no part in leading us here. We will never see such a cross like this one again," I told Sara and was certain of my feelings.

It was nearly five o'clock when the three of us returned to Furth. I dropped Sara and Lisa off at post housing and said, "I'll see you tomorrow at work."

Minutes later, I spotted a honey wagon and pulled off beside the old palace road. The words of Don's friend Hank came to mind. "Look for the honey wagon in the field. The wagon carries fresh honey right from the hive," Hank had commented a month earlier while smiling from ear to ear. The honey wagon brought to my mind Papa's fresh honey from his own bees.

A huge brown horse was pulling a creaking covered wagon through the open fields. I jumped out of the car and ran into the field, shouting, "Hey! Halt! Halt!" The white-haired German hunched forward and ignored me. So I shouted loudly again until the wagon finally came to a full stop. The elderly man looked frightened but said nothing. He trembled all over. My shouting seemingly had scared him to death.

I cleared my throat because of a terrible smell and then anxiously said, "I wish to buy some fresh honey." I gasped from the odor, which smelled like a septic tank that had been filled with years of bacteria and took my breath away, and said, "Oh my." Being a daring young country girl, I took two steps closer to the wagon. "I wish to buy fresh honey," I said, hoping that the farmer understood English.

I did not believe for a moment that the middle-aged German man could not hear me. He was most irritated with me. I thought he had been befuddled by my shouting and was now ignoring me.

The man puckered his lips as though he was ready to say a mouthful. "Nix honey! Nix honey!" he shouted. Then quickly he nodded his head to and fro, pulled the horse's reins, and slowly drove the wagon further into the fields.

Seconds later, I felt lifeless and dreadfully nauseous. "Oh, there's no honey. That man is spreading human feces over the crops," I mumbled to myself. I realized such foolishness of me, as I ran toward my car crying. Indeed, I would get Hank back for such a dirty joke, and that was a promise. Then I thought, *Oh no, I mustn't say a word to Hank. If I tell Hank off, he will tell Don. Dear me, then Don's friends will call me the dummkopf lady of Bavaria.*

Unfortunately, Furth soldiers played the honey wagon joke on their wives. No one had told me about the joke—not even Don. *Today it is my turn to be humiliated*, I thought as I climbed into my car tearfully. The honey wagon in the fields of Germany had never existed. The soldiers in Furth had named the septic-waste wagon a honey wagon.

I uttered words of truth at that moment. "Lord, you are teaching me to be a prudent wife. I shall never eat fresh vegetables in a foreign land as long as I live."

Minutes later, I arrived home. I saw a note and realized that Don had made a short trip to Furth. It said,

> Hello, love! Tom and I came to Furth for supplies. Be home in a few days. I love you so much. Sorry I missed you.
>
> Love Don

As I read the note, I had a feeling that Don would be home if he could be. However, while he was out on field duty, I vowed never to mention alcohol again. I realized that hounding Don to stop drinking was causing him to drink excessively. I was grateful when God inspired me to be silent, and to have faith in Him.

To keep silent daily, asking Don to stop drinking was a new transformation in my life that I never expected. God's grace filled my heart with deeper compassion, and with hope I had never felt before. After all, King David waited silently before God. He said, "My soul, wait silently for God alone, for my expectation *is* from Him" (Ps. 62:5 NKJV). I remembered that it was in silence that the great saints' lives were transformed.

I was also inspired to examine my impish mind. First, I must stop trying to be Don's savior. How could I save Don from his own destruction?

Unfortunately, Don continued to drink much more at beer gardens with his buddies. *Will Don be home tonight? Where is he? Will he be drinking excessively? I must stop these thinking patterns now*, I thought while reminding myself to constantly stay on my spiritual course.

Thankfully, before Don's return home from Berchtesgaden, I meditated honestly on my own personal inventory, and it was not good. Even though I felt my faith was strong, my heart was crushed. This is what I discovered about my life:

1. I must pray to have a contrite spirit and to spend quiet times alone with God. The heart discovers a marvelous feeling when it awakens in humility and empathy.
2. I must remember that words spoken in anger aren't worth the painful consequences they bring.
3. I must pray myself out of resentful moods when Don is drinking. Anger, bitterness, and an unforgiving heart only give glory to Satan.
4. I must come before God and ask Him to forgive my anger. Scripture says, "Better to dwell in the wilderness, than with a contentious and angry woman" (Prov. 21:19 NKJV).
5. I must never quarrel over Satan's brew. Scripture says, "There is one who speaks like the piercings of a sword, *but* the tongue of the wise *promotes* health" (Prov. 12:18 NKJV).
6. I must honor truth, for God is *truth.* The truth is that I have no power to change a spouse who is addicted.

7. I must *trust* that my only hope is to remember this verse: "I will say to the LORD, "*He is* my refuge and my fortress; My God, in Him I will trust" (Ps. 91:2 NKJV).

8. I must never live with an addicted spouse who is physically abusive. Scripture says, "Husbands, likewise, dwell with *them* with understanding, giving honor to the wife, as to the weaker vessel, and as *being* heirs together of the grace of life, that your prayers may not be hindered" (1 Peter 3:7 NKJV).

Thankfully, I came to realize that our Lord has more grace than our own bitterness. As I continually studied His Word, the world around me changed. I was learning to, "Be joyful in hope, patient in affliction, and faithful in prayer" (Rom. 12:12 NIV).

My life changed as the Holy Spirit led me. I vowed that from that day forward, Satan would not receive glory in my circumstances. It was during that time that a deep realization awakened within me. I realized that our heartaches could only be healed by God's love because He is love. I could do nothing on my own to rid myself of the bitterness that I carried. I would continually choose to believe there were miraculous moments through the eyes of faith.

Midday on Saturday, Don returned from Berchtesgaden. I noticed immediately that he was trying to make a good impression. "Honey, would you believe that I drank very little while I was away?" Don shared as he embraced me tightly.

I reminded myself of my self-declared promise. *Act like you didn't hear that. Don't mention the word alcohol,* I vowed. I smiled weakly at Don. I knew that he loved testing my patience on the subject of spirits. I would bite my tongue off before saying the word *alcohol*, which I seldom said in regard to Don's drinking returning from field duty.

Quickly, I forced myself to change the subject as Don took me into his arms again. "Sweetheart, you look so tired," I whispered and then kissed him gently.

Don sighed and set his boots neatly in the corner of the bedroom. "I'm dead tired," he replied, squeezing my hand tightly.

As evening approached, Don retired to bed. I decided to sleep in the guestroom where I wouldn't hear Don's dreadful snoring. I hoped my mind would stop its rambling. *Just one night of complete rest would help my tower of emotions,* I reflected. I had a garden of thoughts, but within the hour, a peaceful sleep welcomed me.

In a spiritual dream, my body floated up and soared into the heavens. Instantly, a place appeared seemingly not like this world. Unexpectedly, a mysterious dark-gray cloud burst into a brilliant light. As I gazed into the light, I had a sensation of heavenly splendor opening widely. Then the clouds slowly rolled away, and a soft light appeared beyond a very narrow pathway.

Where is this place? I wondered, feeling somewhat frightened. Then unexpectedly, the narrow pathway seemed brighter than before. A voice spoke gently to give me instructions: "Walk the pathway. Don't look below!"

As I walked the narrow pathway, I became curious and glanced below. Far below, no life existed. Only thick, dark, vast floating substances swirled below. *Could that be hell?* I wondered.

The voice spoke again, "You may stop walking." I paused instantly.

Seemingly in a flash, I then entered another place. This place was so beautiful and had thousands of lovely flowers that grew alongside the pathway where I stood. The voice whispered again, "You must not pick any flowers. You must only touch them."

The first flower beside the pathway appeared to be a rose. I noticed that it was not like earthly roses. The rose was the deepest red that I had ever seen. It was larger than earthly roses. The second flower was white. It seemed to be a type of lily that was so immense; it would have covered my frail eighty-two pounds of worrisome flesh. I felt this flower drawing me to it like a phenomenal magnetic force.

I stretched out a hand to touch the flower when, suddenly, the flower embraced me gently. Instantly, strength flowed through my body and filled me with a jubilant joy. The flower's superior embrace was incredible. It was impossible to describe all that I felt in that moment.

After what seemed like a short journey, the voice whispered at last, "It's now time to return. Walk the pathway and enter the light through which you came."

Moments later, I returned to the light that I had previously come through. Within seconds, my body floated like a feather through the heavens. Finally, my head touched my pillow. I awoke to realize that the unexplained had taken place in a dream. I wondered with joy why I had had the dream. I realized at that moment, my body and mind were filled with a new strength.

Months went by, but the dream never left my mind even for a day. I felt inspired to research the dream. Surely the flower meant something in the dream. I had no rest within me until I entered the library to research the flower.

Amazingly, the flower that had renewed my eighty-two pounds of flesh and that had given me a miraculous healing was from the amaryllis family. This *Amaryllis belladonna* was from a family of bulbous South African plants and was frequently cultivated and sold as the belladonna lily. However, in the Greek language, the name amaryllis also has a personal name, such as in pastoral poetry. The personal names were *a country girl* or *a shepherdess*.

The flower that had embraced me now revealed my life as a young girl—my love of writing poetry and being a country girl and a shepherdess. I was inspired to believe that God had permitted my dream to show me His love. I believed that the awesome presence in my dream was God's glorious presence. I felt so blessed that I cried for days. It was wonderful to know that we have a God who loves us so much.

During the time my dream occurred, I had told myself to give up on Don's addiction. I had even considered leaving Don. The words that of my doctor, Doctor Thomas, had frightened me: "If you lose any more weight, to the hospital you will go."

More than a month after my dream, things began to fall into place. I began to gain weight, and my appetite flourished. My dream had brought something I had not expected. My spirit, which had felt lament, soon filled with amazing joy after my dream had occurred. The dream had also changed my way of thinking. It was time for me to be a humble Christian and not an angry conqueror.

I made a promise to remember one more thing. No matter what came, God desires His children to think realistically, objectively, and with dignity. While Don was drinking more and was away from home a lot, my personal rights mustn't be overlooked.

How unbelievable, I thought. Just like the sun beaming in its strength, heartaches were teaching me forbearance by God's amazing grace. *How can this be when it hurts so much?* I wondered. Once again, I felt like a butterfly that had been set loose and was now able to fly over towering mountains and the deepest valleys. *Lord, keep my heart soft and gentle,* I prayed faithfully.

Remarkably, I began to see marvelous things happening regarding Don's drinking. The secret chambers of my womanly heart were learning to smile with hope and confidence. I was inspired to believe that the Lord Jesus owned a garden of flowers and abides among them.

My dream had revealed that God's love exceeds our human struggles and that He interceded when we least expected Him to. Though I didn't know whose voice spoke in the dream, I believed the dream was all Gods' plan. It was a dream I shall never forget. My mind and my frail body were renewed by the purest, loveliest flower that I would never grow in my own garden.

CHAPTER 7

I T WAS 1965, and springtime was approaching. The sun shone beautifully. Word spread through Furth that the soldiers were being assigned to extract-training school. Don's friends had already left for field school. Some combat troops left Germany for the States with orders to go to Vietnam for assignment.

I had to use our fuel sparingly. People were worried. The Germans expressed their worry of those who spoke English. I observed that Don and his friends were drinking more than usual. My close friends Sara, Millie, Esther, and Pat were frightened to death that their husbands might go to war. Countless army demands were being given to soldiers. Every soul hates war.

Will Don go to war? I contemplated, horrified at how quickly things could change for every family. Throughout the week, I had a strange feeling that something had happened. I often felt a foreboding. All day, my friends Esther and Katie had been on my mind.

On Saturday afternoon, I heard a knock on our door. It was Don's friend Samuel. His eyes were crimson from crying.

"Has something happen to Don?" I asked as my heart beat rapidly.

"No," Sam answered. He sobbed as his voice gave a ragged cry. "Oh Lord, I've lost them both. Esther and Katie had just reached the border of Florence, Italy, when a terrible landslide hit them. The car was completely buried. Some bodies haven't been found yet. Perhaps by tomorrow, they'll find our car," Sam said, continuing to sob between words.

I could do nothing but hold Joe. God had called Esther and sweet Katie home. Grief overtook me. I could not help but think that if I had gone with Esther to share the driving as she had asked the two of them might have missed the landslide and been alive.

The very next week, the army transported Sam stateside. He had suffered a complete mental breakdown. The army thought that Sam needed to be near his family in Georgia for support and that it would help his recovery.

Everywhere I looked, it seemed as though tragedy was striking. Unfortunately, surviving life's uncertainties was truly getting to me. I also realized that living with a mate who was addicted created a life of excuses. Don's drinking had caused me to lose little pieces of myself. I was beginning to understand that a wife must not live with excuses.

Making excuses for a spouse's drinking is not excuses but a lie. I call these lies the secret things that a spouse is capable of doing when inebriated. Most wives become enablers when surving with addiction. I was beginning to realize, that I had been an enabler making poor decisions. God's Word, was teaching me, there was nothing I could do to save Don from a self-destrictive addiction.

Thankfully after my dream, I realized something else. That all my inner resources I needed was in God's Word. If we serve Christ, he heals our enabling thinking patterns, takes care of us, guides us, and gives us grace and mercy. The Bible says, *"Eye has not seen, nor ear heard, nor have entered into the heart of man the things which God has prepared for those who love Him"* (1 Cor. 2:9 NKJV).

As God's Word taught me through faith not to be an enabler, it was the beginning of a new spiritual life. By faith, we understand, just as it says in the Bible, "Now faith is the substance of things hoped for, the evidence of things not seen" (Heb. 11:1 NKJV).

One night when Don came home, I said to him, "Perhaps God is testing our faith."

He stared at me in amazement. "Honey, haven't you learned by now? You're a wonderful wife. My drinking has nothing to do with you. Yes, I know God will get me," Don blurted out.

It was early December of 1965 when joy filled the air and opened the season for Christmastime. Don knew Christmas was my most precious time. Together, we found a lovely tree and decorated it two weeks early. We spent many weekends around the tree with Tom, Sara, and Lisa.

The Nuremberg headquarters had dismissed all employees because of another major blizzard throughout northern Germany. I watched from the palace's windows as snow fell unceasingly like large popcorn balls. Major Joe glanced at me and then toward the window. "The city will be in frenzy," he commented, taking his coat from the rack in the corner.

People were exiting quickly through the palace's gate hoping to reach home before the big one arrived. Major Joe walked toward the window. "Oh, we better leave now, Carolyn. I've seen blizzards like this. Before long, the city will be impossible to drive in. Crazy! Crazy! Like nothing you've ever seen in Nuremberg," the major said as he gathered up his books.

My pulse quickened because the snow was mounting higher. I knew all about snow blizzards, but the major thought I was unaware of the danger ahead. I glanced at Major Joe. "I am ready to leave now. Sara is lucky to be on vacation," I said to him.

Instantly, I noticed the major's smile became warmer and wider at the mention of Sara's name. "Let's get going," Major Joe insisted, gripping his black leather case.

I knew Don would not be coming home because he had been assigned to weekend duty. With the blizzard going on, he might be asked to remain at the medical unit after duty for emergencies.

I rushed quickly to my car. I was happy that all beer gardens would be closing. "Thank God! Thank God!" I murmured loudly. Everything within my heart wanted to cry out at that moment. Indeed, I hated that so many married soldiers loved to group together in beer gardens rather than go home.

I had been on the highway just minutes when the blizzard took a turn for the worse. I could hardly see through the windshield of the car. Suddenly, I saw something on the windshield and shouted, "What's that beneath my wipers? Oh Lord, it's a parakeet trapped beneath them, flipping to and fro. I must try and save the little fellow right now."

The blizzard winds had blown the tiny creature onto my windshield. The wiper blade had traped its foot. No, I dare not put God's tiny creature through any more pain. I stopped at a red light and jumped out of my car. Quickly, I turned to face the cars behind me and shouted, "Halt! Wait a minute!" I slowly climbed up on the car's hood. It wasn't going to be an easy rescue. Twice, I slid from the hood of the car and fell hard on the street. *Oh, I must keep trying*, I assured myself. Then the cars that had stopped behind me began to honk.

"Oh, I'll save the little fellow this time," I uttered. The cars kept honking for me to get out of the way.

"Call the police," a voice echoed through the air.

I screamed back from the hood of my car while lifting my hand in the air, "Go around me. Can't you see I am trying to rescue a parakeet? I heard Germans love parakeets."

Within seconds, the ice and snow had frozen instantly. I slowly released the wipers and carefully removed the parakeet. The rescue was successful, but I feared the wipers had harmed the tiny creature's leg.

Gently, I brushed the snow from its body and noticed a golden band around its right leg. Its tiny one leg was limp. Its feathers were bright blue, green, and yellow. It was so beautiful.

Suddenly another voice shouted, "That lady is as drunk as a skunk." I assumed he was an American soldier because he was speaking English. The one word that cut my heart was *drunk*.

I shouted back at the soldier. "No need to rush, soldier. All the beer gardens are closed. No happy hour tonight." Then I raised my hand in the air to let drivers know that I was on my way.

Later, I realized my anger had not been caused by what the young soldier had said but by my feelings of frustration, my disappointments, and all the changed plans. I had allowed my circumstances to get the best of me once again, although it had felt good to release my pent-up feelings.

I placed the bird beneath Don's old army hat in the back seat of the car. I made a blanket with my scraf and put it over the hat. I wondered where I would put the tiny fellow when I got home. "You're in the army, little fellow," I said loudly.

It seemed like it was an endless journey from Nuremberg to Furth. Along the way, I named my newfound friend Windy because of the windy blizzard.

Once I was finally home at Furth, I placed Windy inside the kitchen sink and covered it with a curtain, taping down all edges of the curtain to the sink. "You'll be safe until tomorrow," I said. I noticed its leg, was not broken.

I could hardly wait for Don to see Windy. He loved the little fellow at once. Before long, daily Windy watched me like a mother elephant watching her babies.

Two months later, Windy began repeating, "Everything beautiful!" Don had taught Windy those words.

Overwhelmed by Windy's intelligence, I phoned the pet store. "My parakeet talks," I informed the veterinarian. "Why do parakeets have a gold band around one foot?" I asked.

"Oh, parakeets don't talk," the veterinarian replied. "In Germany, we don't mark birds with gold bands. It sounds to me that Windy possibly came from another country," he informed me.

Windy knew when I was at my lowest point too. At those times, Windy never failed to say, "Everything beautiful!" He was a spiritual, constant chirper until I covered his cage in the evening. A few months later, Windy became the center of attention.

A week before that, I had dismissed the maid because she had constantly asked for rationed items. Sugar, cigarettes, and other goods had been on her weekly list. The maid had continually wanted me to ignore the rules of the US government, which had prohibited the army from selling or giving away rations.

One Saturday at noon when I had no shoes on, I reached up to admire my new lamps, not realizing the lamps were possibly damaged from shipment with their wires exposed. Suddenly, a high voltage of electricity shot through my body. My hand bled slowly as I slumped to the floor. A warm feeling of peace flowed through my body. I wanted to rest in it. At last, my mind was able to blot out Don's drinking. Like a cloud moving to reveal the sun, my eyes opened for a second. My whole being desired to call out but could not.

An hour later, I trembled as though my body was frozen. *Lord, have I died? Where am I?* I wondered as I struggled to open my eyes.

"You've been in shock," the tall nurse standing beside my bed informed me.

A tall middle-aged doctor stood quietly beside my bed as well. "Mrs. Keeton, wake up! Young lady, you are very lucky. Be thankful you were not wearing shoes with metallic elements while mopping your floors. Because you were shocked by a high voltage of electricity, it would have killed you instantly," the doctor said, smiling as he walked to the door. "Oh, by the way, Mrs. Keeton, your neighbor Juanita told me that there is an angel living in your house. She told me that a parakeet saved your life," the doctor said, shaking his head.

I didn't respond. Things were not fitting together. Dear me, had I gone completely off my rocker? Had Don's drinking finally wrecked my mind? Maybe the doctor was a little eccentric and that's why he made such a comment. Who in the world would believe Windy was an angel and had saved my life?

Suddenly, Don appeared. He was in tears. "Oh honey, what happened? This is terrible. Trouble has found you again," he said sweetly. Don took in a deep breath. "Love, Juanita told me that Windy sat on her windowpane refusing to leave and danced all around to get her and Raymond's attention. Juanita said Windy refused to go away until she followed him to our door," Don said with a worried voice. He had been frightened by my experience.

Juanita stood beside the bed quietly before saying a word. "Carolyn, we don't know how Windy got out. Raymond cannot explain how your door got unlocked. We know you always keep it locked. Raymond and I knew something was terribly wrong when Windy wouldn't leave the windowpane. We knew Windy never left your side."

Unpretentiously, I uttered, "I am not sure of anything at this moment."

I was sent home from the hospital that evening. Later, I took time off from work while I waited for my hand to heal. I hoped my near-death experience would remind Don how precious life truly was. Don would love me into wellness if he could, but I realized that his craving for alcohol came first, even in the most difficult times.

That evening, Don joined his friends at the club to calm his fear of my near-death experience. The club was his secret hiding place away from me. He did not want me to watch him drink. Most addicted persons have a hideout and feel right at home there.

While recuperating at home, I imagined the flowing springs at Lewis Farm, which were often covered by the earth's rubbish. Beneath the rubbish, fresh living water always flowed. How I yearned for God to remove the nonsense that alcohol created. I wanted to feel love and to be fresh again—fresh like the roses that bloom as they are kissed by God's affection and new life comes forth. That was the way it should be when we served Him. *Why are things not changing?* I contemplated, hoping they would soon change.

Unfortunately, my close call with death brought no new changes. I felt deeply grateful that God had spared my life and was humbly thoughtful about life itself.

God compares our short, temporary life to grass and flowers. How very true this is.

It was about three months later that I wrote down good practices to keep in mind.

1. A godly woman of faith will always give words of understanding. A wife mustn't allow a spouse to be the center of her existence. Every woman's heart must have its own center of understanding to move into divine intimacy.

2. A wife mustn't lie about a spouse's drinking, particularly in regard to family secrets. Truly, a wife living with addiction tells little white lies that lead her heart to sin and embarrassing moments. Promise yourself to never lie against God.

3. A woman of godly faith must wait patiently for God to reveal a new discovery about her. God wonderfully created her. She must be determined to restore her marriage even when a spouse is drinking, if circumstances permit. She is permitted to divorce if there is physical abuse. I desire to be a woman who trusts God's Word and for God to make me whole.

4. A woman's godly faith will let her know that she should not live in the shadows of addiction and experience denial, alienation, anger, self-pity, guilt, fear, or other negative feelings. Such

CAROLYN L. KEETON

feelings keep her soul in bondage while Satan and his demons laugh at her. It is Satan's plan that God's people give no glory to the Lord.

5. A woman's godly faith reminds her that pastoral counseling is important during the trials of addiction. To attain peace in our inner being of strength and power, is confessing our sins to God and accept His forgiveness. Pastoral counseling is also rehabilitating, even to families who do not worship God.

CHAPTER 8

MONTHS LATER, DON'S drinking had become disgraceful. I was heartbroken but still gave thanks to God in bad situations as I had promised to do.

One September morning, Windy's chirping brought back a memory of my wedding day. By now, I was coming to terms with the fact that I was giving up part of my life while desperately trying to survive with Don's addiction. Even so, I still gave thanks to God daily.

Often the words of Jesus reminded me, "As the Father loved Me, I also have loved you; abide in *my* love" (John 15:9 NKJV).

I constantly tried to understand why I worried so much over Don. "Such foolish thinking," I mumbled as I prepared for the day. I quickly opened the shutters as thoughts of the farm rushed into my mind. I visioned the big eagle, soaring Lewis Farm with unruffled peace. How I longed for a home filled with peacefulness and to rid my thinking patterns that occurred constantly because of Don's addiction.

In spite of unsettled feelings, my heart recalled the words of Jesus. "I will not leave you orphans; I will come to you" (John 14:18 NKJV). Such promising words were a welcome sanctuary at that time in my life.

It was late when Don came home that night. My feelings had been right all along. My freaky accident had caused Don to drink excessively. He put his hands around my waist and swung me around and around. He released me and then kissed me. My head spun, but I laughed at him anyway. Don knelt on the floor to kiss my wrapped hand. "Love, your hand will be okay," he said as he struggled to get up from the floor.

Within the hour, Don was almost asleep in my arms. "Get to bed," I insisted, and then he struggled into the bedroom. For a while, I lay awake, listening to the sounds of the people coming and going outside.

First, I want to say that I detest giving glory to Satan. However, I am inspired to share with families that where drugs and alcohol are in homes, Satan's demon spirits join together day and night.

Nevertheless, I slept peacefully for nearly seven hours. At 6:30 a.m. while saying my morning prayers, I heard whispers coming from the corner of my bedroom. In the corner, three huge dark shadows, which were shaped like clouds, stood. What are those things? What are they whispering about? I thought. "Oh God, those creatures are demon spirits," I uttered and watched as they continually whispered to each other.

These three demon spirits had a plan. Suddenly, one of the shadowy figures floated toward my bed. Frightened, I grabbed hold of my bedpost. I could tell that this demon spirit was in charge because it instructed the other two demons not to move. The other two demons applauded my fear and then grunted constantly loud at my nervousness.

The demon approached my bed as I held onto the bedpost. It removed my hands and gently lifted me onto the floor. The demon's ragged body appeared to be coated with a slimy substance. I feared this substance would drip onto my face, but it did not. I covered my face just to be sure. The demon spirit began to slowly embrace me, and somehow, I knew it was going to rape me. I shouted to Don loudly three times, but my cry had no impact.

I shouted out to Jesus, "Help me!" The minute they heard my prayer, the three demons vanished. Of course, I was shaken beyond belief as I struggled to get back into bed.

I knew at that insant why the demons were in the house. A friend and I had blessed every room in the house with my Bible. We had done so the night before my attack. Together, we had prayed in Don's room that any demon spirits would be cast out, for I had been experiencing other attacks.

My feelings may not be accurate, but I believe the demons were trying to get back at me for blessing our house. I had some knowledge about demon spirits during this time. I knew that the Bible confirms that Satan, and his demons are real.

Absorbed in thought, *were the demons already in the house before this event? Did the demons have anything to do with Don having alcohol in the house? Yes indeed, and I have not thought differently from that day forth.*

About two weeks later, I began to experience nightly dreams that convinced me that the three demons had returned to the house. In my dream, twelve ladies were in vintage dresses. The ladies joined hands in a small chapel and prayed together. One of the elderly ladies began to pray for families experiencing substance abuse and drug addiction. The lady prayed these words: "Satan, we cast you out of every addicted home in the name of Jesus!"

Suddenly from the back of the chapel, a loud beastly voice roared like thunder, which hindered the lady's prayer. None of the ladies recognized the language of the demon spirit. Unexpectedly as the demon roared, the chapel trembled as if an earthquake was taking place. Its savage cry was beyond belief. The demon hammered on the tiny chapel walls and was determined to stay there.

"Keep praying! Keep holding hands and pray! Do not break the prayer circle!" the lady instructed the others.

Finally, I awoke from my dream to face reality. Our house was trembling like the small chapel in my dream. The living room walls were being attacked as demon spirits hammered from inside our house. The demon spirits were in the living room, and Don and I were witnessing dreadful attacks.

What is happening? I thought, very frightened, and tried to calm myself. The demon spirits hammered on the front door a second time, and then the house was silent. I thought the demons had left the house. To be certain that no one was pounding on the door, I searched outside at precisely 3:30 a.m. All was quiet, so I returned to my bedroom.

Suddenly, the demons battered the living room walls at least five more times. The demons continued thumping the walls. Then they pounded the front door before leaving the house. As I entered the living room, I sensed an entity of evil in the room.

Suddenly, Don shouted from his bedroom, "What's happening out there? What's that loud groaning and thumping noise? Good grief, do something."

Minutes later, I entered Don's bedroom and looked at him breathlessly. "No need to put your pants on to search outside. The trembling and hammering you heard was demonic activity," I said. I had not told Don about the attack that had happened two weeks earlier, for I knew Don did not believe in evil spirits. Don only stared at me as he shook his head and blinked his eyes.

I said to him, "I know you don't believe demons were inside our house." Then I explained my dream to Don. "The ladies in my dream were praying to cast out demon spirits from homes that have addicted people in them. When I awoke from my dream, our house was trembling, and the door was being hammered. Don't you see, Don, demonic spirits dwell where alcohol abounds. We're witnesses of this truth," I explained as I trembled.

Don looked at me exhaustedly. "What are you getting at? You believe that demons caused that terrible noise?" he asked motionlessly. Don gave me a funny look and then added, "It's impossible to believe what you just said. How can you even prove that demons exist?"

I already knew Don's feelings about demonic spirits. *Hush!* I told myself, knowing Don would never believe that such a horrifying experience was demonic activity. Don and I had attended the Baptist church as young children, but most pastors had never preached on demon spirits.

The Bible tells us that demon spirits roam the earth and that Jesus Himself was tempted by Satan in the wilderness. My experience taught me that demon spirits vanish *at the name of Jesus*. The Bible says, "Be sober; be vigilant; because your adversary the devil walks about like a roaring lion, seeking whom he may devour" (1 Peter 5:8 NKJV).

After yearly encounters with Satan, I received the gift of baptism in the Holy Spirit. This is a gift offered to the children of God, and it turned my life around. I received extraordinary "power from on high" (Luke 24:49) which Jesus promised to His disciples.

Jesus said to them, "For truly John baptized with water, but you shall be baptized with the Holy Spirit not many days from now" (Acts 1:5 NKJV).

During May of 1966, Sara and I sat in the palace courtyard. We were watching a tiny sparrow in her flawless nest. I realized that I was somewhat like the mothering sparrow—always hurly-burly on the inside over Don's life like the tiny sparrow fussing over her little ones.

I waited fretfully at night for Don's return home. I was anxious to talk about the day's events.

Soon the babies were ready to leave the nest. The tiny sparrows were free to go now, and no bird would touch the nest again. No indeed, I would not leave my dwelling place no matter what happened. Often, I thought about returning to Lewis Farm but didn't want to bring grief to my parents.

"God will show me the way," I said to Sara. The two of us watched as the tiny birds helplessly flew onto the next branch. "God watches over us just like those tiny birds," I said thankfully.

"Indeed He does," Sara replied, laughed, and then reached for her lunch pack.

As I watched the tiny birds flying from their nest, I thought of a home without alcohol. The Lord most certainly abhorred drunkenness. The Bible says, "Wine is a mocker, Strong drink *is* a brawler, and whoever is led astray by it is not wise" (Prov. 20:1 NKJV). Don's drinking caused him to separate from God, when he needed His grace the most.

Suddenly Sara breathed deeply. "I have something to tell you," she said dishearteningly. "I feel exactly like that mother sparrow with her babies desiring her attention." Sara choked on her words as tears filled her eyes. "I pray Tom will show more love to me. I feel he has fallen out of love with me," Sara said as her voice faltered.

"Next month, we'll be leaving Germany, and it will be the saddest day of my life. You know that I depend on the major's advice and support so very much. I don't believe I can make it without the major in my life," Sara said, raising her eyes. Then Sara glanced impatiently down the palace courtyard. I could tell she was hoping against hope that the major would join us for lunch.

"Sara," I said, "please trusts God. I know you love Tom deeply. Please don't throw away a chance to make things right."

Sara answered with wide eyes and affection in her words, "Unfortunately, I never had a father growing up, and the major is like the father I never had," Sara said teary-eyed.

"Yes, I know," I replied candidly. "We both know the major is our dearest friend, but Sara, we also know that saying good-bye is the grief of army life."

Sara's eyes filled with tears as she lifted her face to gaze at the sky. I grasped her hands and said, "Sara, you must believe that a woman's virtue is an admirable trait of her soul. Tom loves you the way you are. He would never change anything about you. Tom's eyes are filled with love when he looks at you. I pray you believe that."

Then I added, "I know changes come to our lives, for our well-being is important to God, Sara. God inspired me to keep my silence when Don is drinking, even when he is out all night playing cards with friends. This morning, I didn't say a word. I did slam his head into the vanity cabinet while he was searching for his shaving cream. Don just laughed at me as though it hadn't happened. I know God does not want me to act like that, but I was so angry."

Sara chuckled. "Well, at last! It's about time you cracked Don's brain," she declared with an upturned face. "Knowing how patient you are, I cannot believe that you would do anything like that to Don," Sara said and then laughed as I had never heard her before.

"Sara," I replied, "Life isn't about who is winning. I feel much guilt for slamming Don's head. Often in a crisis, it's difficult for me to obey God's will. Sara, we mustn't give up."

Sara's eyes grew thoughtful and then suddenly glistened when the major entered the palace courtyard. "So here you two lovely ladies are," he said teasingly and took a seat on the bench. The major's smile seemed to calm Sara's unsteadiness.

I thoughtfully speculated, *Oh my, is Sara falling in love with the major?* Perhaps I had overlooked Sara's true feelings for him. Whatever the truth was, their relationship was respectful. I believed Sara's relationship with the major was that of a daughter to her father.

Sara tried desperately to hold back tears, but minutes later, her emotions crumbled. "Major Tom and I will be leaving Germany. Tom's tour ends on July 20th," her words faltered as she caught her breath between sobs.

The major and Sara looked at each other sadly, as the sunshine briefly flashed on their faces. Major's eyes spilled glossy tears as he took hold of Sara's hand. "Things will be okay. We three buddies always knew that parting would come sooner or later," Major Joe said as he reached for his handkerchief.

I noticed that the major's eyes showed signs of his having another rough night. Then suddenly, the three of us were sobbing and could not stop ourselves. Minutes later, I decided to return to the palace's headquarters to gather my belongings for the day.

When I was there, I gazed out the window and waited for Sara to return to the palace for her belongings. Nearly half an hour later, she appeared and said, "I'll drop you off at home." Sara rubbed her eyes and wiped her face in despair.

I recognized Sara's pain. I knew how much she hated to leave Germany. "I'm so glad we no longer ride the old army bus. Thank God, Sara, you're going stateside at last," I said, although I knew the words wouldn't ease Sara's tormented heart.

I thought Sara would stop crying, but she could not get control of her trembling. Sara struggled to her feet and said, "Okay, let's go home now."

On the way home, Sara was silent. "God always does the best thing for us," I assured her.

When I arrived at the house, it was empty. As I was going up the steps, my foot slipped. I caught myself and hurried to the door. Once inside, I fussed over Windy, making sure that I showed him tender love.

Minutes later, our old German phone rang loudly. A mysterious voice came through the receiver. It was a young man who spoke English fluently but with a German accent. "You're beautiful today. I've been watching you," he said softly.

Dear Lord, I thought, *has this man been stalking me?* My heart beat rapidly in my ears.

"I must talk with you alone," the young man said firmly. My stomach knotted as I slammed down the receiver. Quickly, I ran to the door to check the bolt and make sure it was locked.

Within minutes, the phone gave another reverberating ring. *Oh, I must answer it. What if something has happened to Don?* I told myself. I also convinced myself that listening to the caller's voice might help me recognize him. Slowly I picked up the heavy receiver again.

"I won't hurt you. I want to meet you somewhere. I saw you at Soldiers' Field. I also know where you live. I've been watching you a long time," the young man said while breathing heavily through the receiver. Nearly two weeks went by, and calls continued.

Why in the world would a German pursue me? I thought as fear filled my mind. I had been very careful around the men at work. I knew no men at the palace besides Major Joe and Sir Hogg. I had also taken great precautions never to mingle with strangers. In a foreign country, American army wives knew they should be very cautious at all times. I thought to myself, *Stalkers only stalk beautiful women. I am not beautiful. How can this be happening to me, Lord?*

My mind was in turmoil. Once a week, I took my evening walks at Soldiers' Field for exercise. *Well, Lord, I'm in another mess,* was my deepest thought. My disturbed thoughts were only one issue. I must not tell Don, or he would drink more to calm himself. If he drank too much alcohol, anger might be triggered in his mind. "Where is he when I need him so desperately?" I shouted out. It felt good to judge Don. After all, a husband is supposed to be home after duty hours.

Quickly, I closed the window shades and fell exhausted upon the bed. "Lord, I'm so afraid. I must stay calm," I uttered consciously. Then suddenly, I remembered that German authorities had no jurisdiction concerning the American military in Furth. The situation would be more difficult if the authorities refused to help me.

On the other hand, because the man spoke with a German accent, the police might possibly help me. Perhaps other army wives had reported the man to authorities. I also considered the possibility that since the German police headquarters were located only a block from post housing; the police might help in my situation. I knew I should tell Don and tell him immediately. I shrugged. I thought about how he might become very angry. His jealous nature ignited when he drank.

About an hour later, I heard the key turning in the lock. I greeted Don's stern face. "What's wrong, honey?" he asked and then whistled loudly to Windy.

"Honey, I had to notify the German police, and they are on their way. For reasons I don't understand, a young German guy is stalking me," I said, wondering what he would say next.

Don's face flushed red, revealing his temper. "How long has this been going on?" he replied. He was irritated to his soul. "Do you know this demented guy? Perhaps he's employed at the palace? You must know him if he's stalking you," he commented with deep concern.

The doorbell interrupted Don's interrogation. "Are you Mrs. Keeton?" the officer asked.

"Yes," I replied. "Please come in."

The two tall German officers smiled politely and then entered the sitting room. The officers spoke little English but communicated surprisingly well—better than most Germans.

My knees trembled as I said, "This is my husband, Don. We need your help. A German, by the sound of his voice is in his twenties, has been calling two weeks. Often, I hear chimes from a huge clock in the background. He seems to know the places I visit during the day."

Suddenly, one of the officers stretched his long legs and then pampered his blond mustache before speaking. "Mrs. Keeton, German authorities aren't responsible for protecting you. You are an American." Then he said sternly, "The German police have no jurisdiction in matters concerning post housing. Sergeant you know this."

Don drew in a long breath. "Now wait just a minute. This crazy guy is German, not American. You're telling me you can't help? What an unfair system you have in this country?" Don said expressively as he shook his head.

The other officer spoke up, "That's right. We're not permitted to give any protection to Americans; however, since we know the guy is German, we might be able to break a few rules. We'll see what we can do. Perhaps we can catch this guy. However, from what you've told us, this guy isn't an amateur. Your stalker fits the pattern of a very dangerous guy. He's also very skilled. He times his calls when Don is not home."

"He does show signs of being an expert stalker," the first officer agreed.

I glanced at the tall officer with a quizzical look. "Please try and catch this guy," I pleaded.

"Good," the officer replied in well-spoken English. "Let's set a trap for this guy on Wednesday night. Mrs. Keeton, you'll meet the stalker someplace along the old palace road. Please don't worry. We'll be right there when he arrives. We won't let anything happen to you," the officer said assuredly.

Don fired back, "Surely, you aren't serious about such a plan? No indeed, my wife will not be meeting a crazy guy on the old palace road. Anything could go wrong in that area." Then Don added sharply, "You must arrange a better plan than that one."

The officer presented a second plan. "Okay! Let's have Mrs. Keeton meet the stalker in the parking lot outside. Mrs. Keeton, you'll wait in your car for him. We'll set up the plan for Wednesday evening. When the stalker calls tonight, lead him on. Tell him to meet you in the parking lot. Inform him you'll be waiting in your car at 6:30 p.m.," the officer said pleasantly.

Don agreed right away and then said with enthusiasm, "That's a much better plan. Thank God. I'll hide in the basement and watch out the window. If something goes wrong, I'll be close by to help my wife."

Of course we would comply with the officer's plan. Since German authorities owned the telephone services, post-housing phone numbers could not be changed, so we had no other option.

Wednesday the officers arrived before 6:30 p.m., and to go over plans one more time.

The phone rang twice. The officers nodded for me to answer it. It was the stalker. "Yes, I want to meet you too. Meet me in the parking lot where I live. I'll be waiting in my car for you," I told the stalker.

Within minutes, the officers hurried to their dark-green car in the parking lot to hide among the trees. Quickly, I followed behind them down the stairs into the parking lot and fearfully jumped into my car.

"Oh my, it's starting to rain," I uttered and then looked through the side window to make sure the officers were still there. "Thank you, Lord. They're watching closely," I mumbled again. I felt safe knowing Don was already in the basement and could come quickly to my assistance at any moment.

I had prayed that the weather would be nice for the plan, but it wasn't. Just minutes after getting into my car, a downpour began. About half an hour later, fog covered the parking lot like a white sheet. I could hardly see the officers' dark-green car near the edge of the woods.

The fear I felt was almost choking me to death. Several cars passed slowly into the parking lot. The fog was now spreading and turning everything into a dreadful sight. My hands clutched the wheel. I wished I could cancel the plans, but it was too late.

"Lord, I don't want to meet this guy face-to-face," I mumbled to myself. Suddenly, thoughts of the stalker's note, which I had given to the police hours ago, deepened my fear. It had said,

> I saw you and your friend at the cathedral. I was so close
> to you, I could have kissed your neck. You looked so
> lovely in your blue dress today.

Slowly, more fog covered the parking lot, much like the Black Forest had when I had traveled to Germany. "Yes," I whispered. "Perhaps God brought rain and fog so this evil man won't show up."

Oh, if I could only breathe some fresh air, I thought. Even countless thoughts of all the trips I had planned did not calm my fear. Fear was my biggest stumbling block and was locked into my mind. My legs trembled like they had during the snowstorm on the riverbank. A ringing rose in my head as though it might be a serious sign. My mouth felt parched. My eyes refused to stop blinking as they often did when I was fearful.

I prayed again and asked God for calmness. I had been through tough times before, but this was a different kind of fear. "Why did I take such a chance? This is craziness!" I said aloud as I accepted the truth.

Within minutes, Don was three feet from the basement window, and watched my car constantly. "This blasted door is jammed. It won't open. Honey, get out of the car. Run quickly into the house now."

I shuddered as I heard Don's shout. It was impossible to run now. A white Volkswagen with German tags had just entered the parking lot.

"Oh, God, keep your hand on me," I whispered as I lowered my head. I raised my head slightly as the VW turned swiftly and then raced off into the foggy night. Like lighting, the police raced after the VW. I imagined the worst. Would the police be able to follow the stalker's VW in the fog? *Thank God. This nightmare will soon be over*, I thought enthusiastically.

About ten minutes later, Don and I waited inside the house for the officers to return. They had chased the stalker into the city. We heard a knock at the door, and Don answered it quickly. "Did you get the guy?" Don asked the officers.

"Sergeant, we're so sorry. Your wife's stalker is very skilled. He knew all the escape routes. The fog is too thick, and we lost him as he entered the city. I'm sure the stalker knew it was a trap," the officer indicated clearly.

Minutes later, the officers waited patiently for the phone to ring as though they knew it would. On the third ring, the officer quickly grasped the receiver. The stalker warned the officer, "You think you're so smart setting a trap for me. You'll be sorry for this," he threatens hanging up the phone. Minutes later, I sensed what the officer was about to say. "Mrs. Keeton, I'm very sorry. We tried to help you. We can't break any more rules to protect you," the officer informed us, said good-bye, and walked out the door.

Don's face crinkled in disappointment and then grew red as he yelled at the officers who were leaving. "I'll bring judgment on you if something happens to my wife. I find it difficult to believe that German authorities aren't interested in catching this guy." Then he slammed the door.

My mind felt like a leaf twirling about. Did the officers protect the stalker because he was German? Perhaps they allowed the stalker to escape. Possibly, the officers thought I was having an affair with him. My mind would not stop spinning. However, it was true that unfaithfulness in marriages was increasing among military families. The officers were no doubt wise to this fact. I realized at that moment, there was no one but God to protect me.

Don had to work long hours on weekends at the clinic. "Yes, God will protect me," I cried, feeling self-assured that He would.

As the weeks went by, I couldn't understand why Don's drinking was more frightening than my stalker. God had protected me in rough times. I dare not let a stalker frighten me.

"I have a plan for this crazy young nutcase," I said loudly. No human hands would be able to break the lock on the inside of my hand-built bedroom closet. The lock was designed by skilled Germans and had been used for generations. Most assuredly, I would hide there for protection if things got out of control.

I slept restlessly for weeks, even though Don expressed loving concern. Eventually, I convinced him that my stalker had vanished. It was a little white lie that I considered to be absolutely necessary. I knew that Don worried about me. What could he do to protect me? Additionally, his time at the clinic was demanding.

At work, I confessed to Sara and Major Joe that my stalker had not vanished. "You must promise not to go anywhere alone," Sara said pleadingly. "Tom will check the house when Don is away."

My nerves snapped. "There's no protection for American military living in Germany. Sara, you can't watch me every day. God will protect me now," I told Sara, still believing that He would.

It was early summer when the Holy Spirit revealed truths to me. I was learning to trust God in all my circumstances, and Satan knew that well. Indeed, the evil one had found a way to weaken my trust in God and had done so with a stalker. It was an inspiring truth, and I had no doubt about it. I praised God daily for revealing that truth to me.

Therefore, I would pray continually for the Lord's intervention. I would be careful never to go out alone, would stay close to friends, wouldn't answer the phone, and would ride to work with Sara or other friends.

As months went by, I reminded myself, "But the Lord has been my defense, And my God the rock of my refuge" (Ps. 94:22 NKJV). I couldn't wait to tell Sara and Major Joe on Monday about my true feelings. That Monday, I said, "Its God's amazing grace of protection. I feel that He has put me in a big bubble and that no one can harm me," I said with peaceful hope.

The major's face changed many colors, and then he replied seriously, "Carolyn, this guy is sick. Be careful. Your stalker isn't going away. It's a shame that Americans need more protection overseas." I knew that the major gave good advice, and I took him seriously.

"Something should be done about such a law," the major commented with the deepest concern. The major glanced at Sara. "Okay, are you two ready for lunch in the courtyard?" he asked anxiously. The month for Sara and Tom's departure home to America had now arrived. The three of us would never picnic again. Indeed, I would miss Sara, and our hearts were sad.

June of 1965 arrived with a heavenly blessing. The bright flowers of spring brought a golden day as Don entered the house shouting, "Love, where are you? You will never guess what has happened. Good Lord, I never imagined we'd be going home before my tour ended. I still have more than six months remaining for my tour in Germany. Out of the blue, the army gave I and two other soldiers' orders to go stateside," Don swung me around and around.

I looked at Don intensely. "Oh, this is all God's doing," I shouted. "Please believe me, hon. Its God's intervention to take me out of Germany."

Don looked at me and was somewhat puzzled. "Love, why would you say that?" he asked.

I hadn't told him that the stalker was still leaving notes. For a moment, I wanted to tell him the stalker was still harassing me, but I didn't dare reveal that I had deceived him. *God will forgive me,* I told myself.

Don's face flushed seriously, and then he replied, "Perhaps this is God's plan. Sorry, love, we can't go to Italy to adopt a baby. God knows best. Right now, we must focus on packing your fragile items. Please don't worry, honey. The packers will gather the larger items. I feel the future is full of good things," Don informed me with excited anticipation.

CAROLYN L. KEETON

CHAPTER 9

D URING EARLY AUGUST of 1965, I packed small items. Don and I spent the afternoon telling friends good-bye. Having left Germany several weeks before, Sara, Tom, and Lisa were now settled stateside. Nearly all of our household items had been packed and were ready to be shipped. However, there was one more thing left to pack. I quickly placed the small blue sweater set gently in the bottom of my suitcase and gave a deep sigh.

Within the week, another problem arose. The sharp-nosed veterinarian had grinned and then had explained, "You mustn't take Windy to America. Windy won't survive the long flight." So without hesitation, I knew what I had to do. I would give Windy to our friends Dave and Millie.

"Oh, I can't leave my Windy behind," I told Don as I cried. No one could comfort the pain I felt. Just two days later, I told Millie while choking on my words, "Take good care of my Windy."

Millie could not help but cry. "Please don't worry about Windy. I promise to give Windy marvelous care. Dave and I won't let anything happen to him," Millie said as she grasped the hand that was holding Windy's cage.

Two weeks later, our plane lifted off from Frankfurt Airbase and began its journey to New York. As the plane passed through the morning light of Frankfurt, I glanced below. I wondered if my stalker knew I was leaving Germany. I could not help but wonder how my stalker had watched me without my ever seeing him. Had he been hiding in the cathedral? I had been careful as I had entered to pray. I would never know the answers.

Thanks to God, I am free from a freaky, notorious guy, I thought at that moment. "You thought you would win, didn't you? God showed you whose boss," I uttered, squinting my eyes.

"Who's boss?" Don asked. I had not realized that he had heard me.

Nevertheless, I would leave such thoughts behind. Within the day, we would be home in America. I thought about the pilgrims and how they must have felt as they had seen America for the first time. I reflected that their hearts must have fluttered just like mine did at that moment.

At last, Don and I would be home at Lewis Farm and would remain there for two weeks. I worried about Don's assignment to Fort Dix, New Jersey. Would he be there two years? I really didn't know since TV news footage daily informed us of the Vietnam crisis. Don knew that his orders could change quickly as the threat of war progressed.

I gazed out the plane's window and thought about how wonderful it would be to see Lewis Farm again. I realized there was always a special place where God seemed so real to me. My place was where God ushered us into His Presence. Alone in the country woods with God at my childhood home on Lewis Farm had always been that special place.

I knew my heart had not completely forgiven Don. My heart was filled with the betrayal of our love. I was physically well, but unforgiveable feelings hindered my spiritual life. I needed time for my heartaches to heal. Having gone through years of crises because of Don's addiction, I was not the same young lady I had once been.

Should I go to New Jersey? I contemplated. I tried to ignore such vexing thoughts but knew they were real. *It hurts too much to think about the future at this moment,* I thought disquietingly.

Seconds later, a thought overtook my mind. *Miracles come to us when marriage is restored and love is reborn.* I knew God had fearfully and wonderfully created us. Now I must pray for God to help me feel love again. I am sure that every wife experiences such feelings while living with an addicted spouse.

At around midafternoon, Don and I felt overwhelmed by five hours of flight time. I missed Windy already, and my stomach was tied into knots. "We should have chanced bringing Windy with us," I whispered to Don, although I knew Windy was in safe and loving hands.

Don took my hand. "Sweetheart, Windy will be okay with Millie," he replied and then pinched my cheek gently, which was a loving habit he always practiced.

CAROLYN L. KEETON

Later on, warm thoughts of Lewis Farm filled every corner of my heart. The sugarcane mill at Uncle Alto's farm would fill the valley with sweetness. Mom's blackberry pies would be baked. The storeroom would be filled with treasures too: dried beans of all kinds, freshly made preserves, churned milk for butter, and all sorts of vegetables. Papa's pickled corn, which had been pressed in a stone pot, would be bubbling and waiting to become a winter's snack.

The Ohio River, which had been called The River of White Caps by the Native Indians, would be transformed by the dawn's heavenly light. Lumberjacks would be gathering timber in Scioto County's foothills and would be thankful for a beaten path.

Before long, my thoughts brought me comfort as I looked briefly at Don. "Oh, I've missed home," I said as I leaned toward him and shaded my eyes from the morning sunlight. Hesitantly, I cleared my throat and eagerly asked Don, "Sweetheart, what time do we arrive in New York?"

As Don looked at me, his hazel eyes flashed with excitement. "We will arrive about 3:30 p.m. in New York. We'll pick up the car at the port at around 4:00 p.m. Then we'll have something to eat and drive straight through to Ohio," Don said, assuring me. "Love, don't forget I must report to Fort Dix a week from now. We'll need at least a week to get settled on post," Don reminded me nervously as he picked at his fingernails.

The homecoming at Lewis Farm was exceptionally wonderful. My sister, Joan, was now a mother of two incredible boys, Jeffrey and Timothy. Unfortunately, Joan was having major problems with her husband Mark's addiction to alcohol. Mark was a dedicated engineer and a wonderful man at heart. I saw that Joan's life was very much like my own and needed prayer. Therefore, I decided it would be best not to tell her about Don's drinking. Because Joan's marriage was in trouble, I would not bring more burdens to my parents.

After our arrival at Lewis Farm on Saturday afternoon, I hesitantly asked Don to go horseback riding. "Let's go riding," I teased. He looked at me and shook his head no.

Don cleared his throat, chuckling before answering, "You must be joking. I've never ridden a horse in my life," he confessed, seemingly irritated.

I pumped up Don's courage. "I'm much obliged to teach you. Star is a gentle mare. She would never throw you off," I said flippantly.

"No thanks," Don replied, giving me a darting look.

"Don't worry," I assured Don. "Many people are afraid of riding horses." I then yelled to Mama on the back porch, "I'll be back in time for lunch." Then I hurried to the barn.

I could hardly wait to get the saddle on Star. My heart beat robustly. Quickly, I rode to the area where my secret hiding place had been when I was a girl. *Perhaps I might see the angel again;* I thought as my eyes and fixed them on three dogwoods.

Three huge trees were in summer's bloom. I fastened Star to one tree. I recalled the day that I had climbed the dogwood trees. My heart jingled with joy from my delightful memories.

It had been Easter Sunday in 1949. The spring floods came quickly that year. The old church bus could not cross the high waters. This prevented Joan and me from attending church that Sunday. At noon, I climbed the three dogwoods, picked blossoms, and stuffed them into my pockets. Later with Papa's hammer, wood, and wire and my blossoms, I designed a small Easter cross for Jesus. My young heart wanted Jesus to know that his death was really special to me.

For many days, I ran swiftly to the dogwoods to see if Jesus had taken my cross. Soon the blossoms died, and disappointment grieved me. "Jesus, why didn't you come for my cross?" I said as I wept. After days of checking, I buried the cross beneath the pines.

Suddenly, I mumbled, "My cross may still be there." I dug in the dirt with a large stick. I was about to give up when I suddenly hit something. "That's my cross," I shouted as Star shuddered. Undeniably, it was my tiny cross. The wood had almost decayed, but the wire that had been shaped into a cross was still well defined.

I nodded my head in disbelief and embraced the cross like a mother holds her child. I glanced up where I had once seen the angel, and desperation filled my heart. Once I had been a happy girl in my secret place, which had been filled with excitement for the future. Now filled with sadness, I thought about my marriage and considered what I should do.

I had decided that I would stay at Lewis Farm when Don left for Fort Dix. Under the circumstances, I felt this was best because my wounds were so deep that I could not endure the pain any longer. I prayed to God for the courage to tell Don.

As I buried the cross a second time, my spirit awakened. "Who had suffered more pain than Jesus on the cross?" I whispered. *Was I meant to find the cross?* I questioned.

I eagerly raced home for lunch. Obviously, I believed that our marriage was not strong enough to hold together. Heartily and gratefully, I was glad to have found my cross. The cross had renewed my spirit. Christ had died to rid my hurt that I felt deep within. *God graciously gives grace and compassion in our struggles*, was my deepest thought.

A week later, I reconsidered my decision about what course I should take in my marriage. What if I made a dreadful mistake by not joining Don? I knew that divorce would be painful too. Perhaps I should consider Don's addiction as being a sickness. I knew that life became a springboard when living with an addicted spouse.

I saw Don as a husband who always seemed to be away from home. Don saw himself as a very responsible man. He deceived himself by believing that he was intelligent and strong enough to control his desire for alcohol.

It was not easy, but I decided to join Don at Fort Dix and to ignore my painful feelings. Amazingly through my trials, I was seeing the faithfulness of God. "The Lord *is* good to those who wait for Him, to the soul *who* seeks Him" (Lam. 3:25 NKJV).

It had been five years, but I still believed Don's sobriety would come about. Why was God taking so long? He could send angels to defeat Satan's plan to destroy our marriage. My faith continually reminded me to dress in victory each day and to wait patiently on the Lord.

During the month of September, I received a letter from Millie. Windy had disappeared right after we had left Germany. "Who will take care of Windy now?" I said heartbrokenly to Don.

Don's eyes grew sad. "I pray nothing will happen to our little fellow. Please, honey, stop worrying. I know Windy will find a new home," he replied tearfully.

I wept for days in the dimming twilight as worried thoughts filled my mind. What if Windy didn't find a home? What if being eaten by a wild animal was his fate? How inconceivable it seemed that after leaving Germany, Windy had vanished.

My mind went into a spin. Dear Lord, suppose our friends had been right. Maybe Windy had been an angel in disguise. "Get a grip on your mind," I uttered to myself as I remembered Windy's faithful chirping words, "Everything beautiful!" Not only did I remember them but also was reminded daily of the excellence of God's works. "He has made everything beautiful in his time. Also He has put eternity in their hearts, except that no one can find out the work that God does from beginning to end" (Eccles. 3:11 NKJV).

Although my friends believed that Windy was an angel, I found no proof in the Bible that angels came to earth as tiny creatures. However, I was convinced that Windy had indeed proclaimed his rank as an angel by saving my life.

CHAPTER 10

A FTER OUR RETURN to the United States, I prayed faithfully that Don would give up drinking. I thought that being stateside again might help. I felt that because we had endured inharmonious years in Germany, Don would realize that alcohol was affecting his health. Shortly after arriving at Fort Dix, New Jersey, Don began drinking considerably more, and my heart felt the deepest pain.

As extraordinary as it may seem, I experienced another spiritual dream during that time. My dream reoccurred at least once a month for more than a year. I was the keeper of my dream and didn't share it with family and friends. Friends saw me as an outgoing young lady leading a normal life. I was employed in Princeton, New Jersey, at a wonderful data processing company for Princeton University. My coworkers never would have thought a phenomenal event was taking place in my life.

Thankfully, I realized that spiritual dreams were transforming my life. I was inspired to examine the worth and purpose of the dream. I felt that my dream disclosed my heartaches and frustrating experiences. I was inspired to believe my dream was all about my *heart*.

In the dream, Don and I had bought a huge Victorian house near the city. I had selected the most beautiful wallpaper for each room. During each noon hour, I invited twelve unknown guests to tour this newly decorated Victorian home. As I approached the last room on my tour, the door was locked. I struggled exhaustedly to open it, and soon the door opened.

I turned to invite my guests to enter, only to realize they had vanished. So I entered the room. The room was murky and dim. This murky room brought tears to my eyes. All the furniture appeared to be for children, but it had been displayed dreadfully around the room.

Faintheartedly, I observed a fireplace filled with spiderwebs. It looked like a scene from a horror movie. My beautiful wallpaper had peeled away from the walls, and only sticky paste remained dripping off the walls.

"Dear me, my labor was all in vain," I cried uncontrollably. I wondered what was happening to the beautiful paper on the walls.

Then suddenly, the door to the room closed, locking me inside it. *Oh, I must open the door!* I thought but could not get it open. I was haunted with fear and confusion when I thought the door might never open.

I prayed that my dream would cease but was convinced it must have a purpose. I was inspired to believe that God wanted me to truly search my heart. I longed for a home that was free from alcohol, for God desires home to be a peaceful place.

In the dream, the door I struggled to open was the door to my heart. I knew that God knocked at the door of our hearts and wants to carry all of our burdens.

There is a healing fountain next to the heart of God. The Lord desires to heal us from all lofty thinking that comes against Him.

At that time, I felt no matter what comes in our lives God desires we have a joyful heart. I believed the murky darkness in the room, was the sadness of my heart. Once again, my heart had lost its joy. One day, reading Psalm the joy of forgiveness, "Be glad in the LORD and rejoice, you righteous; *and* shout for joy, all you upright in heart!" (Ps. 32:11 NKJV)

Later, that is exactly what I did in rough times. I sung to God with praises. He also taught me a lesson for my well-being. "A merry heart does good, *like* medicine, but a broken spirit dries up the bones" (Prov. 17:22 NKJV).

I realized that laughter lightens the heart. Somewhere along the way, I had lost my merry heart. Outwardly, I appeared to be happy, but inwardly, Don's drinking dominated my thoughts constantly. I felt that Satan was manipulating my thoughts, by causing animosity toward Don.

Don came home very tipsy. At dinner, I served him three pork chops, but he demanded another one. I left the kitchen to pull myself together. Suddenly, Don threw his plate toward the kitchen window.

CAROLYN L. KEETON

The greasy plate ruined my kitchen curtains. In that moment, my hurt and anger covered my being like nothing I had experienced before. Don had never thrown things before. It revealed how frightening his anger was.

I was inspired to believe that Satan would love it if Don and I would fight, for the devil influenced my mind with lies.

Indeed, Satan's craftiness was deceitful. He tried to convince me that Don could do worse things than drinking—another crafty trick he tried to pull.

I imagined my angry feelings, as being like a mad honeybee sipping sap. I was inspired by the Holy Spirit to give belly laughs at Satan, and my anger to God as an offering. My faith reminded me not to grieve the Holy Spirit. Scripture says, "Be angry, and do not sin: do not let the sun go down on your wrath, nor give place to the devil" (Eph. 4:26–27 NKJV).

Don felt sorry for throwing the plate and asked for my forgiveness. I could not deny the truth. I must be willing to forgive Don or our marriage would not last. What a blessing to remember the words of Jesus: "Forgive and you will be forgiven" (Luke 6:37 NIV).

In April of 1967, Don's assignment at Fort Dix changed suddenly. He received orders to go to South Korea. It would be his second tour there. Wives couldn't go to Korea during that time.

Don couldn't wait to tell me our future plans. "Love, I will not leave you. My reenlistment will be next year. I'll finish my army retirement with the army reserves," Don commented as though he would miss the army terribly.

The news lifted my hopes. I thought that perhaps civilian life would bring new beginnings and strengthen our marriage. There was only one thing that gave me assurance. *Keep trusting!* My spirit whispered. "*It is God who arms me with strength, and makes my way perfect*" (Ps.18:32 NKJV).

Within the year, Don had signed all his army reserve forms. He was excited about life. He got a job at Scott Paper Company and worked there faithfully for more than a year. Then Don sought employment with the US government in 1967 and was employed there until he retired.

We bought a lovely, small ranch house. I envisioned with new self-confidence that our new home would be in the East Coast. Even though I was content, it did not take me long to realize that a fine home with beautiful surroundings does not stop a spouse from drinking when he is addicted.

On a beautiful summer day in 1967, I was remembering God's promise at Saint Lorenz Cathedral. The thought of God's promise never left my heart. One day I said to Don, "Our children will be born here," as he shook his head pitifully. Although we had been married seven years, not once had I doubted that God would keep his promise to me.

At the end of June, I waited impatiently at the doctor's office. I truly had no idea what the doctor was about to say. I had been feeling somewhat tired and had had cramping at times.

"You're going to be a mom," Dr. Johnson said with a deep grin on his face.

My eyes overflowed with tears. "I am pregnant! I am pregnant!" I shouted, shivering like a goose in water. "I can't wait to tell Don," I uttered, as a weakness filled my body. Rightfully so, the day had swallowed me up, and I had not been prepared for it.

That evening, a June shower refreshed me as I took my usual evening walk. I patted my flat stomach with hope that the doctor's diagnosis had been accurate. *A baby will change things,* I told myself. "Don will believe God's miracle now," I mumbled as I walked fast and breathlessly. I felt as though my mind was in the clouds. "Don will be a loving dad," I uttered, pushing away all doubt as I continued my mile-long walk.

I could not help but wonder if Don would take me seriously when I told him about our miracle. After all, he had endured years of hearing the word *baby* and not seeing it happen.

Later that night, I smiled at Don as he took off his shoes and rubbed his feet. "That's better," he groaned. I watched as Don quickly and neatly placed his shoes in the closet—one of his many upright traits I respected.

CAROLYN L. KEETON

My words were soft and low. "Honey, I went to the doctor today. We're going to have a baby. No, I'm not imagining it," I said as my words bubbled over.

There was a long silence in the room before Don spoke. "Dear God, are you sure? You cannot be serious," Don answered as his face took on a superior smugness.

I could tell Don didn't quite believe me as his face grew thoughtful. "It's okay, honey. Reality will hit us soon," I said, flushing with joy.

As I spent time alone in the quiet hours of the day, I felt that the things we were thankful for came by having a thankful heart. My heart felt so very humble. Of course, I knew that the thorns of addiction were real. Just the same, God waited to hear my words of thankfulness.

Filled with joy, I realized that God had kept his promise to me of motherhood. His grace had turned around my life in a day. Deep inside, I knew Don might continue to play cards and chugalug at night. Still, my miracle was the beginning of a new life for me. I would deal with trials to come in a peaceful manner.

How amazing it felt to have my spirit soar with abundance higher and higher and like an eagle with unruffled calm. My womanly soul had received a miracle from God. His matchless grace filled my mind and body. *How can the Lord Jesus love us so much?* I wondered daily.

Momentarily, I pictured the eagle at Lewis Farm, which was so confident of its flight in life. I knew at that moment that faithless feelings would never enslave my mind again. I was confident that the demon spirits that abide with the devil's brew would never mentally or physically intimidate my life again. I knew this healing I felt was from Jesus. Peace at last, just as the Bible says, "The Lord will give strength to His people; The Lord will bless His people with peace (Ps. 29:11 NKJV).

The following day, I phoned Joan to share my miracle with her. "God has granted me peace at last. Just imagine, I am going to be a mom," I said jubilantly.

Joan replied as though countless thoughts were on her mind. "Sis, I pray daily for my bitterness to end. Mark's drinking has nearly crippled my life. I believe God will change my situation too," she replied with humbleness.

I bonded with Joan's agonizing distress. "Sis, things will work out. Just keep your faith strong. When God wants things to change in our lives, they do. Our very survival depends upon our Lord and Savior," I encouraged, knowing her deepest pain.

One evening, I reached for the small blue sweater set. "See, honey, I bought this years ago in Germany. You never knew this because I kept it a secret," I confessed.

Don drew in a breath joyfully and then let it out slowly. "Oh, I can't believe this is happening to us. A baby will change our lives. I must get my act together and stop all this crazy nonsense," Don confessed as his eyes widened with the deepest joy.

"I know you're going to love being a dad," I assured him and was certain of my feelings. Deep inside, I knew that a baby would not put an end to Don's addiction.

Lord, please keep my faith strong. Thank you for the precious gift of motherhood, I humbly thought as I took the small sweater from Don's hand and embraced it.

On January 10, 1968, at Sacred Heart Hospital in Chester, Pennsylvania, I looked on as Don dressed our son, Dean, in the small blue sweater set. My eyes filled with tears as I remembered the day that I had bought it at the baby shop in Germany. At last, the small box sat empty upon the bed beside us.

I watched as Don's face gleamed when he held eight pounds and six ounces of love. His face flushed with the pride of a dad who was consumed with love and admiration. No words could express our feelings at that moment. God had promised that we would be parents, and at last, it was a reality. I made certain that every button on the sweater was in place.

"What a beautiful son we have," I said to Don as I noticed his tears.

Don could not speak for a moment but then he replied, "I can't believe he's really our baby. He is really ours."

Unbelievably and once again on July 30, 1970, a miracle took place. I gave birth to a precious daughter, whom we later named Kateri. It was also during this time that Sister Theresa Maria came into my life. The sister visited me unexpectedly one Saturday afternoon. She stood beside my bed at the hospital and searched my face before she spoke consoling words.

"I just visited your baby girl this morning," the sister remarked, raising her eyebrows. "Mrs. Keeton, I noticed you haven't named your little girl yet. Perhaps you would consider the name Kateri. She looks so much like a Native American. She has such beautiful black hair and eyes," the sister commented.

Then she added, "As I visited the library this morning, the Holy Spirit spoke to my heart. I was inspired to give you this book to read. It is titled *Kateri of the Mohawks*," Sister Theresa remarked as she handed me the book. "The Holy Spirit also revealed to me that you have a strong faith. The Kateri in the book is a woman of faith," the sister commented and nodded her head.

How in the world could Sister Theresa have known about my life? I wondered. My eyes filled with tears. "Yes, sister, I believed God for my children, but how do you know these things?" I asked, choking on my words.

The sister squinted her eyes and then replied," Mrs. Keeton, our heavenly Father reveals many things to us. Please read the book. I know it will inspire you to name your little girl Kateri." The sister's eyes gleamed as though she had accomplished her saintly mission. She smiled fantastically and then patted my hand gently before leaving the room.

I noticed the sister's face had been filled with tranquility. *I cannot believe the sister knew about my life,* were my deepest thoughts.

Indeed, the sister's words revealed to me. If the Holy Spirit had spoken to the sister at the library, then it was the Holy Spirit who had spoken to me at the cathedral when He had said, "Some day, you'll have children."

The sister's visit inspired me to believe that God truly speaks through others. Our hearts are inspired forever by their words. I also wondered if the Holy Spirit had revealed to the sister that I was experiencing personal crises.

The next morning the sister visited again with smiles, "The Holy Spirit spoke again to my spirit, that you're having personal struggles. I must pray for your well being, and your family. Oh yes! "One more thing," the sister said before leaving my room. "The Holy Spirit also revealed to me, that you have traveled over many waters."

That moment, my spirit thought joyfully, *"How could the sister have known these things about my life, except of by Holy Spirit?" Dear me, must I tell Don about Sister Theresa?* I wondered. I convinced myself that Don would never believe such an event had taken place.

At that moment, I passed into a new phase. I would keep faith alive unswervingly. How blessed I felt as I realized that it was God's grace of motherhood that had wholly changed my life. I now felt confident to face the future as a new mom. Determinedly, I opened *Kateri of the Mohawks* but then closed it quickly to read later.

At that moment, I felt my mind fill with peace. Thankfully, I was free from bitterness. My innermost self, had discovered a powerful breakthrough. I found myself praising the Lord even in baffling times. I realized what a miraculous deliverance from bondage I had received because of God's grace. I was also inspired to believe that He had chosen Sister Theresa at just the right time to help us name our beautiful daughter.

Then my wondering mind calmed. With a spine-tingling inquisitiveness, I picked up *Kateri of the Mohawks* and began to read without interruption.

CHAPTER 11

J OYFULLY, I CHERISHED every precious moment of being a new mom. I daily saw Don's overflowing love for his children. There were priceless moments when he played marbles with Dean and gave piggyback rides each night. He truly believed God's gift to us had been a miracle and shared those words with his friends.

I realized that Don's life, even though he was an addict, had indeed been exceptional. Thanks to God, after ten years, there was no need for me to try to change Don's mind-set when it came to drinking. The erratic feelings that came from trying to save an addicted mate could be wretched. I was inspired to let my feelings of annoyance pass quickly. This was not an easy challenge, but I followed God's leading as I put my faith and trust in Him.

In time, I learned that alcoholics have genetic traits. They differ from others in self-assertion, attitude, responsibility, maturity, and other personality traits.

I gave thanks to God that Don always displayed a positive attitude. He worked daily, was kind, and never started fights as some drinkers do, was totally dedicated to the army reserves, and held many achievements in the army. Indeed, he was different from most alcoholics I had known throughout my life. Like millions of addicted people, Don lived constantly in denial of his addiction to alcohol. I recognized that the turmoil inside Don came out as a pervasive sense of self-possession. Even when Don was inebriated, he usually slept peacefully.

During 1989, Don's health slowly declined. He developed edema in every part of his body from alcohol. He weighed 285 pounds mostly from the fluids in his body. Don's family thought he had gained weight by eating too much, but it was from alcohol. He had developed heart disease and diabetes. It was apparent that he was slowly killing himself.

I have to focus on being a good mom, I told myself. It was extremely important to be a strong, healthy-minded mom. I prayed that Don would recognize his decline and give up alcohol. Sadly, like most addicts Don was in denial that Jack Daniels' was the reason for most of his conditions.

Don always taught the children the difference between right and wrong and that bad behavior did not go unpunished. Don's denial let him believe that he was showing good examples even when he high. Unfortunately, all those addicted to the devils' brew contaminates godly example in our children's lives.

Through time, I realized that it was the family who suffered spiritually and emotionally when loved ones were addicted. Children suffer with anger, that a loved one was in denial and was destroying his or her precious life.

Eventually, I recognized that teenagers who have no spiritual direction become filled with bitterness and dysfunctional feelings. When a young adult endures fear, guilt, and irrational anger, self-pity will overcome him or her. Unfortunately, teenagers feel tormented because they cannot stop a parent from drinking. Teenagers usually express this as hopelessness. Often, teenagers develop negative thinking patterns, which fruitlessly take over their lives. I perceive that those patterns can destroy a family. I witnessed this in my own family generation to generation.

Thankfully, when children are taught God's Word, it enables a family to live with hope for the future. I have known countless teenagers whose father or mother was alcoholic. I never met one who felt positive about the future, and that hurts me. I have known many teens that have committed suicide because they couldn't stop drinking.

Often, I cry when I think about our dear friend who at age thirty-two, gave up hope and committed suicide. My brother Kenneth became addicted to alcohol at a young age. He was a brilliant brother and a loving dad. He worked very hard as an environmentalist. His wife, Christine, loved him dearly and so did his four children. Ken passed away nearly six years ago.

Throughout my fifty years, I have discovered that most wives who do not know God's Word live with anger. Some wives die with their anger. Sadly, young adults find it hard to love the alcoholic until their anger is put to rest. The Bible will teach us how to forgive and forget when bitterness overcomes us. How grateful I am that God's Word gives knowledge and direction to every purpose in our lives.

From dawn until sunset, we will never know real love until we experience the benevolence and mercy of God. It is so real. How gracious He is. His compassion is all-sufficient. We learn this truth through the depths of dreadful heartaches and circumstances.

During 1978, I begin to research a nine-year study on alcoholism. Daily, books on philosophies, occultism, and anti-Christ religions of blasphemy toward God.

Don was still drinking every night except on Sunday. His legs were unbearable to look at. Two of Don's alcoholic friends had died, and their families were heartbroken. Our children wondered if their dad would live to see them reach adulthood. They loved Don so much, and worried about him constantly.

I felt it was time to face the monster that destroyed everything in its path. With a heavenly calling my research studies included alcoholism, world religions, healing by ancient philosophers, ancient mysicial religions, and others. I became addicted to research.

I will never forget November of 1978. I was thirty-nine years old. I was happy as I prepared for my first family Al-Anon meeting. By now, I loved my job at (American Life Insurance). My close friend Helen was my supervisor. That day it was my turn to drive.

I said to Helen, "Could I borrow your red wig to wear to an Al-Anon meeting?"

"Of course," she replied. I shared my plans with Helen. I wanted to be sure that no one at the meeting would recognize me and inform Don about being there.

It was a cold December night. Dean was nine, and Kateri was seven. I had arranged for Miss Thomas to watch the children while I attended my first family Al-Anon meeting. I kissed them both good-byes as they played with their dog, Sarg, near the Christmas tree.

I was excited to meet women *who* felt the same as I had once felt. I was happy to meet wives and hear their opinions about their lives.

I discovered that AA's beliefs grew out of Phineas Quimby's beliefs in the early 19th century. New Thought movement of (Higher Thought) most of which are incorporated in the International New Thought Alliance, led people to the occultist beliefs.

Quimby's (1802–1866) religious theory of human selfhood by way of Christian Science declared that the *sacrificial death of our Lord Jesus Christ* is untrue. My heart was saddened; for it is irrational for any true believer of the Bible to imagine any recovery without our Lord Jesus Christ.

AA's New Thought religious organizations are based on their own ideas of the Bible. These include roots to eastern mystical contemplation. Its ancient wisdom was established by notable luminaries, whose metaphysical beliefs were promoted to heal people's lives.

In time, I realized, *these phenomenal attributes teach people how to have faith in a higher power*, as I glanced at *The Little Red Book* I had just purchased. "The Al-Anon program is the best," as I listened to others. Indeed, I found most books were helpful regarding human thoughts and attitudes.

Suddenly, the Holy Spirit brought alertness to my spirit about *The Little Red Book*. How could I as a born-again Christian call my God a tree, a higher power, or anything else I decided that He was?

In time, I observed that the healing concepts in Twelve Steps are tremendously different from what the Bible teaches a person about spirituality. I had learned that Jesus Christ restores our lives by giving Himself to us.

He is our heavenly Shepherd. Isaiah 58:11, "The LORD will guide you always." Jesus who says, "These things I have spoken to you, that in *me* you may have peace. In the world you will have tribulation; but be of good cheer, I have overcome the world" (John 16: 33 NKJV).

In time, I realized that systemic methods of healing through mental processes brought about self-realization. Psychologically, a person could learn to control emotions by reconstructing his or her thinking to produce positive results. Of course, in A-Anon Twelve Steps people develop spiritually as well as character concepts.

This is wonderful! I thought to myself. *I must have been wrong*, I told myself. A mind-curing movement is teaching people how to live a good, spiritual life, and this is a good thing.

AA's religion views life as a source of God's omnipresence and cocreation with God. First, a person must understand that, one's own conscience brings about mental and spiritual healing. This certainly meant, as a *non-Christian* practice. 2 Cor. 4:4 NAS, "In whose case the god of this world has blinded the minds of the unbelieving so that they might not see the light of the gospel of the glory of Christ, who is the image of God." One example was Bill W. Wilson while writing *Twelve Steps and Twelve Traditions*. Bill confessed that the *spirits* (the devil) were guiding him, he informed to his friend Father Dowling. Why did Bill think the *spirits* were helping him? During the writing of his Twelve Traditions, he was practicing *spiritualism* as a lifelong interest.

We understand that the term *higher power* refers to religion, belief in divinity, and a system of beliefs. Like AA's belief system, it honors universal beliefs of all religions.

Those beliefs include all non-Christian. Oh yes, AA's religion will let you know we are going to talk about God, but any other name is acceptable.

In Al-Anon Twelve Steps, it felt wonderful to see wives no longer crying. Indeed, New Thought's philosophy was changing many lives. I noticed wives emotionally and physically controlling their habitual thoughts about their spouse's addiction. I had experienced those habitual thinking patterns, and they had once been my worst enemy.

As we live with loved ones who are addicted, our thoughts become twisted, and we will welcome any advice. I realize that Twelve Steps, helped to make good decisions through mind control to overcome a person's negative thinking.

In time, I gained insight related to Don's drinking patterns. I realized that Don suffered self-condemnation and remorse being addicted. Of course, the most difficult thing for me to admit was that Don had a *disease*.

Undeniably, Bill Wilson's Twelve Steps included a form of idealism. AA's idealism is the practice of forming ideas, and living with those ideas in one's mind.

I realized, for sixty-years I have never known one alcoholic with *sobriety* that did not believe they would always be an *alcoholic*. Truly, that is a form of idealism. Idealism is a philosophy practiced daily by millions in the Twelve Steps.

Bill Wilson also believed the teachings of psychologist William James's *The Varieties of Religious Experience*. William James once commented, "A God who can relish such superfluities of horror is no God for human beings to appeal to. Is not the man-like God of common people?"

Thankfully, it is in God's Word that we learn to think realistically and not to question life as it should be or how we wish it to be. God's unending *grace* is bigger than all our heartaches and circumstances. We must, always learn to trust and believe that the love of Jesus Christ is unconditionally steadfast in our lives.

Soon, my spirit filled with deep conviction. I knew in the eyes of God for Bible-believing Christians, it is sinful to be involved in misguided biblical beliefs. For reasons I didn't know, God inspired my heart to remain in Al-Anon. I realized that in many ways, the principles of optimistic mental discipline helped one to focus more on the *self*.

Years ago, I had endured low self-image. I felt so grateful that through the Holy Spirit's guidance, my life was restored. It does not happen without heartaches and perseverance. It is all about God's *grace* turning our hurtful memories into gentle and calm havens.

As time went by, I observed that a practice applied through mental discipline inspires a person to search deep within. One example was focusing on *self* to bring about feelings of accomplishment. The practice of mind discipline helped people realize that their loved ones were addicted, no matter what they tried to tell themselves. I couldn't accept Don's so-called disease; for I believed if Don came back serving God he would be healed. Don's addiction spiritually blinded him. Don realized years ago, that God had healed him from his stuttering.

Unconsciously, apart from Jesus Christ, Satanism and the occult with AA's philosophy of mind-control systems, rule people's hearts. The psalmist awakes our hearts with truth: "My flesh and my heart fail; *But* God is the strength of my heart and my portion forever" (Ps. 73:26 NKJV).

In Al-Anon, my heart often wept silently. Seeing others in tears bothered me emotionally. I had once had a stony heart and understood their heartaches. Faithfully, I prayed for each teardrop and desired to tell others that Jesus longed to heal their broken lives. Unfortunately, churchly beliefs were not permitted to be discussed at meetings during the early years.

AA has various organizations with intelligent notables leading them. These "churches" of the cleansing of the consciousness deal with life-changing circumstances. I observed that most people in Twelve Steps believed that God was a higher power and was good.

One afternoon, God reminded me of Isaiah's prophesy: "These people draw near to *me* with their mouth, and honor *me* with their lips, but their hearts is far from *me*. And in vain they worship *me*, teaching as doctrines the commandments of men." (Matt. *15*: 8–9 NKJV).

Nevertheless, the lives of people in the Twelve Step program were changed for the better. *How can this be?* I thought to myself. Those experiencing feelings of abandonment celebrated high levels of personal growth. *What a joy to witness lives springing up one step at time,* I thought as I was touched by women's lives around me weekly.

Then one day, I grew dispirited again. Why Bible–believing Christians participate in practices that have been established by occultists to build up the human will? In my spiritual journey, I pray daily to live humbly before the Lord. Scripture says: "But He gives more grace. Therefore He says: *"God resisists the proud, But gives grace to the humble"* (Jas. 4:6 NKJV).

Undeniably, Twelve Steps indoctrinates people to believe that negative thinking patterns are in the mind and that positive thinking brings about whatever we desire or expect with a proud heart for the future. AA's religion is to love others unconditionally and to teach and to heal one another. Indeed, alcoholics love to help others. I told myself, *that's good. God desires us to love unconditionally.*

During the summer, I realized the Holy Spirit was putting truth in my heart. The *truth* was that AA's New Thought Religion did not accept the Bible's truth of heaven and hell. *Hell* was only a state of mind and not a burning place that God had prepared for those who did not accept eternal salvation in Jesus Christ. *Heaven* is our good works and deeds, and by a true cleansing of our higher consciousness here on earth.

A year later, my heart asked, *Should not true believers give honor to God with reverence in AA's Twelve Steps program? How does God feel when AA's religion believes diseases are basically caused by incorrect thinking? Perhaps, why A.A. doesn't encourage people for medical treatment?*

Limitless times, the Holy Spirit spoke to my spirit about being healed by the mind's power. "This *is* the word of the LORD to Zerubbabel: 'Not by might nor by power, but by My Spirit,' Says the LORD of hosts (Zech. 4:6 NKJV).

Spiritually, my spirit was inspired to pray for Twelve Steps. Should true believers of the Bible be involved with the beliefs of karma, Buddhism, or Hinduism to know their fates or destinies? Indeed not.

AA's religion is rooted in all those beliefs and other untruthful biblical creeds. AA does not believe in a biblical true God as its higher power but a *power* greater than oneself. Such beliefs open the door for Satan to enter our hearts and lives. Indeed, the evil one is waiting for you and me. Please keep your heart open to *truth.*

Bill W. Wilson announced at his meetings in the early years, "The real founders of Alcoholics Anonymous were Professor William James and Dr. Carl Jung." Through the philosophy of pragmatism, James justified the idea that allowed one to assume belief in a god and to prove its existence by what the belief brought to one's life. William James's pragmatism dishonored the Almighty God. Unbelievably, that belief is acceptable in recovery—any strange new gods as a "higher power."

In time, I realized that Twelve Steps spirituality used crisis that was related to past experiences to transform a person's future. Besides that, I questioned what true Christian could believe AA's New Thought

Religion, which believed that divinity dwells in each person and that all people are spiritual beings. *Wow*, I thought, *how we wish that could be.*

The Bible teaches that every human being is born with Adam's nature—that of a sinful human being. We have uncontrollable hearts that want to please themselves.

Throughout the years, I realized that alcoholics became disciples of selfhood. I knew some people who attended AA meetings three times a day and disciplined other alcoholics.

Unfortunately, Bill Wilson's plans for his own religious beliefs are working for millions of people around the world rather than trusting God's Word for recovery. AA's religion totally rejects Jesus Christ as Lord and Savior, which are New Thought's belief.

Please, let's never forget the Bible says: "Therefore, let all Israel be assured of this: God has made this Jesus, whom you crucified, both Lord and Messiah" (Act 2:36 NIV). *Does this not confirm the spirit of the Antichrist?* I told myself thoughtfully. I had learned in the most difficult times that Christ makes righteous judgments in our lives.

God's Word teaches that every part of our being should believe in Jesus Christ, and our lives will grow spiritually. Let's remember the words of Jesus: "I and the Father are one" (John 10:30 NIV).

CHAPTER 12

I WAS LEARNING that I could live a powerful life through the Holy Spirit. God graces our lives with simplicity in spite of painful memories. The Lord Jesus clothes us with God's consciousness—His Word within us. Becoming God-conscious means that there is one God and one truth. God heals us, nourishes us, replenishes us, forgives our sins, and gives us eternal life through faith in Jesus Christ.

With great expectation, I learned that as I gave reverence to God, prayed, and studied his Word, my spirit was renewed daily. I was so thankful, that God waited patiently for me when I often failed to read His Word. I realize God's peace will reign in our hearts, when we read His Word. David the psalmist says, "Your word *is* a lamp to my feet and a light to my path" (Ps. 119:105 NKJV).

I learned something else: If we fail to trust God's Word, we depend on liberal pragmatic organizations to solve our problems in life. That is how life is in a broken relationship with addictions.

Ultimately, in Al-Anon word *powerless* troubled my spirit endlessly. The Bible teaches: "Keep your heart with all diligence, for out of it *spring* the issues of life" (Prov. 4:23 NKJV). In time, I realized that religions that practice *powerless* thinking and repeat this thinking over and over are using brainwashing.

Indeed, to think powerlessly is a destitute feeling that alters one's personal convictions, beliefs, attitudes, habits, and so on. Why would true born-again Christians want to admit they are powerless over alcohol? When we live with loved ones addicted, we have hopeless feelings at times. There is healing in God's Word: "He gives power to the *weak*, and to *those who have* no might He increases strength" (Isa. 40:29 NKJV).

I came to realize that powerless thinking gave no glory to God. Let God's Word encourage you: "Yet those who wait for the LORD will gain new strength; they will mount up with wings like eagles, they will run and not get tired, they will walk and not become weary" (Isa. 40:31 NAS).

It was most important I gave God reverence in the Twelve Step program. However, I could not imagine that this higher power was the God of my Bible. Our God was not a tree, clay beneath our feet, or whatever this higher power was. God's people are to give praise, honor, and respect to our Heavenly Father, who is our Creator.

The Holy Spirit revealed to me that millions of people in Twelve Steps programs would never be healed until they accepted the *truth*—such as how deceitful and dishonest it was to betray God's character or to be involved with religions that believed in human divine existence on earth without *God's Kingdom* which shall be on earth someday.

The essence of our faith as Christians depends on a person's belief in God without the need of certain proof. By faith, we believe and trust in God. We believe that He is real, even though we cannot see Him. Our innermost beings are renewed and transformed by the Holy Spirit. We pray with faith and have pure intimacy with God.

Of course, I believe that millions of people in the Twelve Step program pray faithfully to God. Sadly, New Thought Religion does not profess any essential beliefs of the Christian creed. It also misrepresents God. A person cannot be one with God because God is divine. Therefore, when you think about step eleven—reaching a conscious contact with God—please remember that AA's New Thought Religion believes that those who manifest a higher consciousness represent *heaven,* as the mystics and other ancient religions believe. The Bible is clear about the *New Jerusalem* to come. The LORD says, "For behold, I create new heavens and a new earth; *and* the former shall not be remembered or come to mind" (Isa. 65:17 NKJV).

As years passed by, Donald's addiction became worse. He continued drinking nightly at the club while I pursued my search of alcoholism. I was still employed at ALIC and still secretly made time to attend Al-Anon meetings at night.

Often, I cried on the way home from meetings. I saw wives with broken hearts who shared how their husbands had fallen off the ladder. I met two Christian women who believed in the life of Jesus. "And Jesus went about all Galilee, teaching in their synagogues, preaching the gospel of the kingdom, and healing all kinds of sickness and all kinds of disease among the people" (Matt. 4:23 NKJV).

New Thought's philosophy with its ancient religions focuses on the qualities of inner life, such as prayer, meditation, cocreation with our Creator, being responsible for our own thoughts, and higher-reaching goals. Even so, its religion disavows people's healing through the Lord Jesus Christ. Moreover, it disclaims that Satan has any part in our lives and that people are ignorant and unwise to even think about *evil*.

I often wonder *do millions of alcoholics realize that Satan is real.* For more than fifty years, I witnessed that when alcoholics were drinking, most had no fear regarding Satan. Most in recovery fail to realize, we all fall into Satan's seed of deception.

Deceptively, New Thought's belief is like Buddhism through levels of consciousness, right living, believing, and peace of mind through meditation in which a person reaches the ideal state of nirvana. What is nirvana? In Buddhism, it is the state of absolute felicity characterized by freedom from passion, desire, suffering, and so forth. Through one's uplifted consciousness, new thoughts will emerge and then mature.

In Twelve Steps, epiphany (realization) awakens to which a person reaches a higher consciousness. In this dimension, people reach a rare moment of understanding. For example, in recovery, people reach a state of right living and realize their own *denial*. One will assume that they have had a spiritual awakening, and will become spiritually minded of a higher power. Just as in the state of nirvana, through uplifted consciousness, alcoholics will in time, reach a state of *sobriety*.

Because I wrote and loved poetry, I had read almost all of the biographies of the poets. Ralph W. Emerson was a famous Unitarian, writer, and poet. He was also once a preacher who studied numerous oriental beliefs. Buddhism inspired Emerson's belief in higher thought. His poetry is widely used in Twelve Steps recovery. Sadly, Emerson had put a way his Bible to become the foundering father of transcendentalism.

As true believers of the Bible, it is of the utmost importance to examine our lives by God's Word. "Beware lest anyone cheat you through philosophy and empty deceit, according to the tradition of men, according to the basi principles of the world, and not according to Christ" (Col. 2:8 NKJV).

Month after month, thoughts scrambled inside my mind spiritually and emotionally. Those I believed to be trustworthy led souls away from the Lord Jesus and not to Him. More than this, New Thought's religion denied that people were born with original sin. I believe that it is because of sinful nature, that healing is often detained in our lives.

Let's remember the words of the Apostle Paul: "Christ Jesus came into the world to save sinners—whom I am the worst" (First Tim. 1:15 NIV). AA's relgion believes that people have no *sin*, *Satan* does not exist, and *hell* is only a state of mind in life's heartaches. *Heaven* is to bring into being co-creating; for there is no original creation. *Healing* is enriched by the conscious realization of our past experiences, thoughts, words, and deeds. I wondered, *what are we hoping to become ourselves? Are we to show we are living a better life? Are people seeking God's will among other gods to achieve a life of sobriety but never know to ask God, "Create in me a clear heart, O God, And renew a steadfast spirit within me"* (Ps. 51:10 NKJV).

Most certainly, a practical American spirituality changes lives. It gives direction and support to those who are psychologically bruised and broken. People are filled with compassion for the alcoholic and find acceptance as well. It helps the alcoholic evaluate his or her relationship with our Creator, along with other helpful sources. Lives are being changed spiritually and emotionally for people who never knew God at all.

I realized that expressing my true feelings was a valuable part of having a happier life. Through constructive thinking, people developed visualization and a positive attitude. Regardless of these principles, it is sinful before God as oneself to practice metaphysics in its various forms involved with Satan's occultists.

During certain seasons, God captured my attention again by His Word: "There shall not be found among you *anyone* who makes his son or his daughter pass through the fire, *or one* who practices witchcraft, *or* a smoothsayer, or one who interprets omens, or a sorcerer, or one who conjures spells, or a medium, or a spiritist or one who calls up the dead" (Deut. 18:10–11 NKJV).

I am inspired to believe that New Thought's Religion will satanically influence lives. Why do I believe this? AA is acceptable to "any god," and systematically these forms of divination are enshrouded in these occult beliefs around the world.

Spiritualism is the belief that spirits of the dead communicate with and manifest their presence to the living—a belief practiced by Bill W. Wilson. Reincarnation is the birth of the soul in successive bodies and the belief in such rebirth. Eastern transcendental meditation is the belief that there is a higher reality and greater knowledge than what is manifested in the human mind. It divides reality into a realm of spirit and matter. It was developed by Plato and other great thinkers.

Through God's love and time, I came to realize that self-punishment was a choice that we made. Self-punishment is Satan's plan to blanket people in self-pity and bondage. I have never met one person with an addicted spouse who did not endure self-punishment. I eventually determined that Satan made self-punishment a perfect misery in homes with addiction. It takes years for families to realize, that self-punishment had nearly destroyed their lives. Ironically, it took twenty-five years before my self-punishment finally vanished.

When I learned that Satan's power was not strong enough to prevail against God's Word, I received a miracle. In the middle of Satan's trickery, chaos, and brokenness, the words of the psalmist are so real: "As far as the east is from the west, *so* far has He removed our transgressions from us" (Ps. 103:12 NKJV).

I consider that Al-Anon's spiritual philosophy is a system of philosophical concepts to help people meet their problems in a calmly perspective way. We cannot achieve true happiness practicing occultist philosophies. Our supreme happiness in life is to know God's love within our hearts. Spiritual philosophy simply grows distant and lonely. It has no quiet whispers. The Holy Spirit whispers to us, "My love endures forever."

Indeed, people in Twelve Steps programs achieve hope for the future. However, religions like the New Age god do not teach the heart, only Jesus Christ heals one's innermost being. Those of us who accept Christ as our Savior feel His love living within our hearts.

I reflected in quiet disclosure. *Does healing linked to ancient philosophers indicate a quest for truth?* I was mindful that most ancient philosophers did not practice Christianity or believe in it. Further, occult philosophy helped to establish the foundation for social order. Those truths lay heavily on my mind that year.

Then unexpectedly, I felt that God might bring judgment upon AA's religion. A practical American spirituality believes that continual rebirth (reincarnation) is God's gift. Therefore, humanity will rule, and souls will become immortal. Shrieking, I shut my eyes as visions of the pharaoh and his gods traveled through my mind.

The Bible says that there must be no ungodly practices between God and us. Therefore, metaphysical ideas for healing in the spiritual sense are based on self-love as opposed to the love of God. *That's me!* I reminded myself.

In God's love, we are disciplined. The chain of defeat is broken. How amazing that when we live in God's love, self-pity cannot chant to our hearts.

In spite of disappointments, I never doubted God's timing. Even though I felt time had enslaved me, I trusted that He would free Don from an addicted life.

Countless years when I was unable to overcome feelings of anger, this Scripture always came to mind: "Let all bitterness, wrath, anger, clamor, and evil speaking be put away from you, with all malice" (Eph. 4:31 NKJV).

Other thoughts abundantly filled my spirit. The Lord Jesus will restore any cherished moments that have been stolen because of addiction. The Bible says: "Though He (Lord) causes grief, *yet* He will show compassion according to the multitude of His mercies" (Lam. 3:32 NKJV).

As time passed by in Al-Anon's program, I realized a country girl like me and highly intelligent individuals (almost all of us) desire to know ourselves well. People pray to believe, to accept, to trust, and to have faith in God—or some source of a higher power. Even so, AA's religion believes that Jesus was only a great example, people have no salvation, and there is no Trinity. How God must weep. Christians, let us bow on our knees and pray for AA's churches, which challenge God's almighty sovereignty for His People.

The Lord Jesus is with us through during unspeakable suffering. Amazingly, He always tries to get our attention. Seeing a red bird refusing to leave the lawn reminds you that God has given the bird wisdom to guard its nest. At Easter season we think of the *legend* that the Dogwood tree is what Jesus' cross was made.

I believe God gives each of us a unique identity, even in brokenness. Think about this. In our heartaches, does not our Lord bring out the best in our lives?

In time, my heart questioned that if a practical American spirituality was so spiritual, why did it oppose God's *salvation* for His people? Most certainly, lives become dysfunctional when we try to survive with loved ones who are addicted. AA's philosophy and its traditions, helps people to fully define or comprehend irrational thinking. The Steps teach a person to focus on selfhood, and one's own mental displine becomes reinforced.

Even so, metaphysical idealism mind-controlling techniques are contrary to biblical truth. Its real passion is total immersion in divinity and mysticism itself. That belief refers to absolute being or divine nature—I am God or God is within me.

I am inspired to believe that AA's "I am an alcoholic" is derived from its religious belief regarding divine nature. After all, Bill Wilson instituted those words, and they still apply today at meetings. It does cause the heart to wonder, does it not?

New Thought World's Religions, devised by Satan will not heal us in the tragedies of life, nor should we ignore William James's belief in mysticism: Mysticism is a religious belief based on union or communion with a deity or divine being; outside of religion, mysticism is applied to cryptic, obscure, or irrational thought, which leans toward mystery and wonder rather than logic.

The Bible teaches that there are no spiritual truths apart from God's Word, which is *absolute truth*. Most self-help organizations in the world, such as mind-cure movements have roots to mysticism. Bill Wilson was influenced by William James's belief in mysticism, which is Satan's dark world and does not instill knowledge of divine truths to God's People.

Bill doubted eternal *salvation* through Jesus Christ. This I know, his wife Lois did not believe in Christ or *salvation*. Most importantly, we must remember that false gods deceive us from truth and lead people astray.

My heart grieved that perhaps Bill Wilson died, and Lois non-Christian that Jesus Christ died for humanity. No, they did not enter the portals of heaven, if they did not receive eternal salvation in Jesus Christ.

The beautiful thing is that the Holy Spirit guides us into truth. When we live with loved ones who are addicted, we need a spiritual cleansing within us just as King David says: "Blessed *is he whose* transgression is forgiven, *whose* sin is covered" (Ps. 32:1 NKJV).

I believe New Thought organizations around the world; Satan is drowning people in their thoughts. Millions of people believe quantum physics can free us from lying, adultery, alcoholism, and gambling and can teach them how to discipline their children.

AA's New Thought churches are a mixture of many ancient beliefs. Those beliefs have achieved a far broader intention. A person can become a spiritual healer by taking study courses. Such practices consist of karma, Buddhism, Hinduism, and teachings of personal responsibility.

How are such courses attainable today? They come through practical American spirituality. These materials with basic principles about metaphysical interpretations of the Bible help people know there is one God—the universal mind. God is self-existent, an eternal creator, a sustainer, and a ruler of life and the universe to come. How in the world could any true believer imagine our sovereign Lord appointing human beings to be divine cocreators on earth? Let us remember the words of the Lord Jesus: "I am the vine; you *are* the branches. He who abides in *me*, and I in him, bears much fruit; for without *me* you can do nothing" (John 15:5 NKJV).

New Thought's belief of pantheism gives no glory to God's throne of grace. Pantheism is the doctrine that the whole universe is God or that every part of the universe is a manifestation of God. It is also the worship of all gods and is made up of various cults, such as what was found in the Roman Empire.

Inwardly, I believe a pantheistic belief system is part of Satan's kingdom. The Lord's Word never changes: "You shall not go after other gods, the gods of the peoples who *are* all around you (for the LORD your God *is* a jealous God among you), lest the anger of the LORD your God be aroused against you and destroy you from the face of the earth" (Deut. 6:14–15 NKJV).

A pantheistic belief system is a counterfeit spirituality, which believes that persons can worship all gods. True Bible believers honorably accept the words of Jesus: "God *is* Spirit, and those who worship Him must worship in spirit and truth" (John 4:24 NKJV).

I believe that in the Bible, we discover ourselves and the overwhelming presence of the Lord Jesus in our lives. AA's New Thought doctrine does not refer to Jesus Christ as the Son of God. Although some religions referred to Jesus as a man or a prophet, the Bible says that it is imperative to worship Jesus Christ as God in the flesh: "For God so loved the world that He gave His only begotten Son, that whoever believes in Him should not perish but have everlasting life" (John 3:16 NKJV).

In time, Twelve Steps never convinced my heart that Don's addiction was a *disease.* So true, that God's Word speaks louder than our human feelings about alcohol: "Do not get drunk with wine, for that is dissipation, but be filled with the Spirit" (Eph. 5:18 NIV).

Eventually, I did not feel anger and pity without cause. Why didn't Alcoholics Anonymous adopt the God of the Bible? Why did its religion continually support occultism, spiritualism, and other anti-Christian beliefs? I pondered this respectfully before God.

John 7:24 reminded me, "Do not judge according to appearance, but judge with righteous judgment." Judging righteously in truth, a practical American spirituality teaches simple facts about life. Its golden rule is to build composure, self-assurance, self-control, and serenity and to make recovery a formula throughout a person's life. In addition, it allows a person to live according to his or her *religious freedom.* That is what AA's New Thought Religion, with its universal mystical law of higher consciousness, is all about.

Eventually, these apostate churches of higher level of consciousness will unite world-wide with New Age, One World Religion. The Bible clearly prophesies that the church of the end times will be characterized by apostasy. These ant-Christ religious movements will succeed for a period of time, when the Antichrist forms his world religion on earth. I thought, of the saints who had suffered and died horrible deaths proclaiming the testimonies of Jesus Christ and the prophets who foretold the Bible for us.

Although time and time again, addicted loved ones break our hearts into tiny pieces. Of course, we are dispirited at times, but there is grace and mercy in the words of the psalmist: "God *is* our refuge and strength, a very present help in trouble" (Ps. 46:1 NKJV).

So true, that often God takes time to heal us. I waited twenty-five years for Jesus to heal my wounded heart. It is all about faith, trust, and keeping our confidence in God's promise: "He heals the brokenhearted *and* binds up their wounds" (Ps. 147:3 NKJV).

Indeed, through practices found in spiritual philosophies, we learn the love of wisdom and the search for it. Undeniably, philosophies teach us to think like others, such as in Twelve Steps. We focus on the word *disease* rather than depend on the Word of God. Spiritual philosophies fill a place in our hearts that God alone deserves.

I reached a time in Al-Anon when *The Little Red Book* was like a Bible. As I searched my heart, I was confronted by the truth. The Bible told me that the truth would set me free.

One day, the Holy Spirit spoke to my heart and reminded me that I was not created like Cheerios in a box. Just as we know that no one person is like another, God created each and every soul to be different. In AA's programs, people suffer differently, think diversely, and love in a different manner. Some have weak faith, others have firm faith, and some are atheists. In spite of that, people in Twelve Steps formulate inner consciousness and adapt to think just like others.

When I realized, we cannot save an addicted spouse, nor can we save ourselves. Often in the thorns of addictions, we feel like a tiny caterpillar in its dark cocoon. Then suddenly, its wings burst into a beautiful butterfly of God's Creation. In Christ, we're strong and His love is beautiful! When we are serving the Lord, we see the world in His light. I often wonder why tears fill my eyes when I read this psalm: "For the LORD Most High *is* awesome; He *is* the great King over all the earth" (Ps. 47:2 NKJV).

I became dispirited during my years of research. I broke out with painful shingles when God revealed hidden secrets, which only He knew. I wondered if people in Twelve Steps realized what God said about occultist beliefs: "Have nothing to do with the fruitless deeds of darkness, but rather expose them. It is shameful even to mention what the disobedient do in secret" (Eph. 5:11–12 NIV).

We must faithfully put away *other gods* and serve the *Lord* only. Somehow, someway, we must never stop growing in Christ, our Lord and Savior. Thankfully, the essence of our being is found at the foot of His cross.

Therefore, the Lord is pleased when we examine our hearts. Because AA's religion denies *Jesus's claims of deity – that He is God. Do* you have a higher power without *Christ*? Does a higher power guide your Twelve Steps or Satan? No indeed, we have no higher power if *Jesus Christ is rejected as God*. Millions in Twelve Steps have left their church fellowship, believing all they need is Step principles to make life complete. The Second Epistle of John says, "Whoever transgresses and does not abide in the doctrine of Christ does not have God. He who abides in the doctrine of Christ has both the Father and the Son" (2 John 1:9 NKJV).

My heart was burdened that Antichrist churches did not accept the doctrine of our Judeo-Christian beliefs. Thankfully, the Bible confirms that there will be global Antichrist denominations that will shatter the name of Jesus Christ:

> Dear friends, do not believe every spirit, but test the spirits to see whether they are from God, because many false prophets have gone out into the world. This is how you can recognize the Spirit of God: Every spirit that

acknowledges that Jesus Christ has come in the flesh is from God, but every spirit that does not acknowledge Jesus is not from God. This is the spirit of the antichrist, which you have heard is coming and even now is already in the world. (1 John 4:1–3 NIV)

In the course of time, I realized that Don's love for all people was remarkable for an addicted person. *With such deep love in Don's heart, surely God will free him,* I thought.

God had taught me that He brings order to chaotic situations. Of course, I often felt discouraged. Even so, spiritual changes came accordingly as I allowed God to pursue my heart. I honored the leading of the Holy Spirit never to let the children see me drowning in low self-esteem. Thanks to God, I accomplished my goal. I also made a promise never to speak maliciously against Don in front of our children—one of the worst mistakes a mom can make while surviving with an addicted spouse.

God faithfully spoke to my heart and told me to trust in Him. Presently, this Scripture confirmes my accomplishments, "Those who trust in the Lord *are* like Mount Zion, *which* cannot be moved, but abides forever" (Ps. 125:1 NKJV).

I also realized Don was struggling emotionally over his health daily. I thought that was a good sign because he was seeing that alcohol was killing him. Don was struggling with his spiritual life as well. He began to ask for prayer when I left for church on Sundays. "Hon, please say a prayer for me." I recognized that his voice was sincere. That was a sign of change in Don's life.

In 1980, Donald and I had been married nineteen years. I was forty-one, and Don was thirty-nine. It was almost the Christmas season. The snow was gone, but gusty winds were extreme. I watched out my bedroom window as a tugboat plowed through icy waters, making its way up the river to Philadelphia. "Lord, life is often like a tugboat," I uttered. *Oh, how the trials of life toss us about,* I thought with jumpy nerves.

Later that night, I watched quietly as the children played around our tall Christmas tree. Their dog, Sarg, rose quickly to chase them. Dean was twelve, and Kateri was ten. *My miracle babies,* I thought, giving God praise for my miracle. Don was still in the army reserves and was out with a friend. At last, my plan would come to pass, and my heart was bursting nervously. Don was scheduled for extra duty that night, and my plans were working well.

"Okay, Mrs. Wynn, I am leaving now. Watch the kids," I said as I gave them both a big kiss. *Dear me, where's my red wig? It's in the car. What's wrong with my mind?* I wondered with sheer determination. Once again, I had borrowed a red wig from my friend Helen. Certainly, no one would recognize me and inform Don of my attendance.

It would be my first "I am" open meeting. I would make my grand entrance as a redhead. The meeting was to be held in the hospital's cafeteria, which was two miles from our newly built townhome. Along the way, I thought of the wives in Germany—how provoked the wives had become because of their spouses' dependence. Some women searched clubs and checked to see if their mate was with another woman. Wives drug their spouses out the door by their ears. Often, some women beat their drinker until they left the club. Others grabbed their spouse's paycheck and hurried home to the children. Wives played the peeking game by checking on their spouse.

Within ten minutes, I entered the hospital's cafeteria. The "I am" open meeting had not begun, so I quickly spotted a seat at the right side of the room. I noticed that the seats were lining each side of the room, and people were having heart-to-heart conversations quite loudly.

Then about halfway to my seat, a mighty force embraced my whole being. I felt as though I was somewhere frozen in time. The people who were seated no longer existed. No voices chattered as before. Only silence filled the room.

It felt like I was attending a funeral. *Where did all the people go?* I wondered. *Oh my, am I having a stroke?* I thought seriously. Suddenly, words came through my spirit, "Look toward the front of the room." I felt this must be God's intervention but was not certain. I wanted to leave the room, but my feet felt as though they were glued to the floor.

As I glanced toward the front of the room, I saw a vision of eight or possibly twelve men sitting on what appeared to be a wooden bench.

CAROLYN L. KEETON

A smoky background appeared around the men. *My goodness, are those men smoking?* I wondered as I saw the amount of smoke.

After a brief moment, the smoky atmosphere vanished, and a brilliant light embellished the men. I clearly observed that the face of each man was tainted with tears. As they sat side by side, they twisted and pulled on ropelike chains to free themselves from bondage. These chains encircled the men's shoulders and stretched down to their hands and feet. Bloody scratches appeared on their bare chests. Their faces grew faintly red and then faded to gray as they struggled to free themselves from the chains.

I felt like my heart was going to stop beating. Tears rolled down my cheeks, but I could not raise a hand to wipe my face. I desired to look away from these men, but my head would not budge. I began to weep and observed that the men desired to open their mouths but were too mummified to do so.

As I breathed uncontrollably in what I imagined to be minutes, the vision vanished. Instantly, I realized that people were chattering just as they had before the vision. The room was now in order, and the chairperson was about to speak.

I hurried from the room and threw up in the restroom to calm myself. At this time, I had no knowledge that the Holy Spirit bequeathed religious experiences in born-again believers' lives. After being sick, I quickly left for home. My experience caused me to realize how enslaved Don and those who suffered addictions were. After my vision, I never again judged a person who was struggling with an addiction.

God also answered my prayer. I had felt that Don's addiction had started as a lifestyle. Through the men's faces in the vision, I came to understand Don's bondage. However, it did not change my mind about one thing: Alcohol and drugs were Satan's instruments, which he used to destroy people's lives around the world.

After the vision, I felt so much compassion toward others who suffered alcoholism. My deep-seated thoughts about alcoholism being a disease changed. It was the first time I felt free from thinking; *Don could stop drinking if he truly wanted to.*

I thought about my brother Kenneth's alcohol addiction. What a wonderful brother he had been. Ken had reached the point where he had been vomiting blood, falling down on the lawn, driving intoxicated and fracturing bones.

In 1999, I spoke with a First Assembly clergyperson who told me that Teen Challenge Rehabilitating Center for Drug and Alcohol Abuse had an 87 percent recovery rate. By now, that record has likely increased. How was this amazing record achieved? It was achieved by trusting and believing the Word of God.

I would like to share a few words about my youngest brother, Danny, who died tragically after being stung by a swarm of bees. Our dad had been a beekeeper his entire life. One Sunday morning before church, Dad asked Danny to go with him to check on a friend's beehives. Unfortunately, Dad had sprayed the bees, and they did not like it. The bees came out and attacked Dad. Danny rushed to rescue Dad. Within seconds, the honeybees sensed Danny's sweet shaving lotion stinging him to death. He died half an hour later. Two months later, our father died from recurring cancer.

I am sharing Danny's life for a divine purpose. All who knew Danny saw that his mission was somewhat like the Apostle Paul's. Danny was a true witness of the gospel of Christ. For more than twenty years, his life's work had been to witness to homeless alcoholics on the streets of Tampa, Florida. Sometimes, Danny was ushered away and warned that his life was in danger. Still, nothing prevented the calling God had laid on his heart.

Faithfully, Danny gathered food for the homeless as an opportunity to read the Bible to them. He expressed for many years that the Holy Spirit had not once let him down. He shared that before his arrival in Tampa, God had always prepared an alcoholic who was ready to hear the gospel.

Danny shared the following words with our family countless times throughout his life:

> Most alcoholics do not object to my reading the Bible to them, although many homeless people turn their heads,

not wanting to hear God's Word. Often war veterans are bitter, feeling the world has forgotten them. Others feel their families have cast them aside. The problem is they fail to understand God's Word has the power to heal us. I am convinced Satan has deceived every heart of those addicted to drugs and alcohol.

After Danny's triumphant death, I read scriptures that he had marked in his Bible which he had quoted to the homeless in Tampa, Florida. I am sharing these scriptures to honor Danny's Christian service throughout his life. For those in recovery, please keep these verses close to your heart:

"But I will restore you to health and heal your wounds," declares the LORD" (Jeremiah 30:17). Isaiah 41:10: "So do not fear, for I am with you; do not be dismayed, for I am your God. I will strengthen you and help you; I will uphold you with my righteous right hand."

It was November of 1999. After Danny's death, I remained in the small town of Wheelersburg, Ohio. My parents had sold Lewis Farm and its resort lake and had bought a ranch there. I missed, not being with our children home in the East Coast. I felt so blessed that I had lived to see what a devoted daughter and son God had given us. They had hearts filled with spiritual kindness; they were dedicated to their jobs, no drugs or cigarettes. Indeed I was counting my blessings daily.

Joan and I had trying times. Mark and Don drank until they could drink no more over the death of Danny and our dad's slow decline.

That morning, the winds whistled as I said good-bye to Don with a kiss. "I have said good-bye to your dad. I'll not be returning for his funeral," Don informed me with a weary sigh.

"That's okay," I replied as I stared into Don's eyes. His face was puffy from crying and daily drinking. I noticed Don's face gleamed with excitement, because he would be seeing our children. Before I could say another word, he drove into the morning sunlight.

Later that night, I realized that Lewis Farm would never be harvested again. It had been a painful decision for my parents to sell the farm.

They had shared their lives for more than seventy years on 225 acres near Great Meadow Road.

The state had purchased the farm and the resort lake. The resort lake had been in our family for years. It had been where the kids and I had gone on vacation. Lewis Lake Resort held wonderful memories for all the Lewis families. The state used Lewis farmlands for a wildlife reserve. Hundreds of acres of new pine trees were planted.

Joan's son Timothy now walked in Papa's footsteps. He had obtained seven acres of Lewis farmland. Tim was a crafty builder and had built a rustic dream house for his son Brent and daughter Ashley on high land that overlooked the valley.

I could hardly wait to see the old Lambert farm. I recalled a picturesque scene of its setting sun, which had appeared as beautiful as a rainbow in the early evening hours. The sun's rays were like colorful ornaments, which shot forth from all directions. I gathered my thoughts to discipline my springboard emotions. I thought about how much I loved Lewis Farm.

A few minutes later, Joan seemed determined to let me know that the farm had changed. "The state has scaled nearly every beautiful tree in sight. We will never see all of those beautiful wildflowers again," Joan informed me in a sorrowful tone.

"I want to visit the farm anyway," I replied as I remembered how it had once looked. *Surely, the farm is not all barren,* I thought to myself.

I watched as Joan swiftly sorted through our father's medicines. "Okay. After dinner, we will visit the farm. Mama will attend to Daddy while we're away. First, we will prepare mama's cranberry salad for Thanksgiving," Joan said as she filled the bowl with whole cranberries and fruit.

Within the hour, the two of us had arrived at the farm. Deep down, I knew the real reason I wanted to visit the farm. I wanted to see if the state had destroyed my holy tree and could hardly wait to find out. "Oh my, the beautiful trees that once shaded the farmhouse are gone," I said brokenheartedly to Joan. Together, we walked toward the old well.

I shook all over when I spotted the big family oak. "There it is, sis. I cannot believe it. The holy tree hasn't been touched," I said jubilantly. Soulfully, I thanked God for sparing what my young mind once thought to be a holy tree.

Joan looked at me and gave me her sweet smile. "Well, you see, sis, the angel tree is still standing."

I reminded Joan what Papa had once told me. "Sis, daddy planted this oak tree the day that you were born. Right here is where Daddy tied the nanny goat. Each morning at dawn before going to work, he milked the nanny goat. Because you were just two pounds at birth, the doctor told Papa you had to have goat's milk. Without goat's milk, you might not have lived," I said to Joan and gave her a firm hug.

Later back in Wheelersburg, I sat silently remembering our father's words from long ago. "When I make my journey to the happy hunting grounds, I wish to be buried here," he had said and had pointed at a huge white cedar. Because the farm had been sold, I wouldn't be able to honor his wishes. *Oh, how I wished I had not promised Papa this*, I thought in the morning hour.

It was two days until Thanksgiving, and I was determined that Dad would eat. "We are having our scrumptious Thanksgiving feast early," I said, giving him a hug.

Papa stared through the window with his eyes fixed on a big maple tree. Its bright golden beauty reflected in the sunlight as leaves fell one ... two ... three ... twirling to the ground.

I watched the expression on Dad's face and somehow knew he longed to be at the farm. Slowly, Dad ate a bite of Mom's favorite pumpkin pie and forced himself to swallow it.

"Daddy, you can certainly eat a little bit more," I pleaded. We were heartbroken as Joan and I helped Papa to his high-backed chair.

It was a small thing for Joan and I to nurture Dad as millions do out of love and devotion. Ultimately, we decided to sleep in Dad's bedroom to impart special care. Faithfully night after night, sis and I prayed together. "Lord, send an angel to comfort all of us." Being disloyal to God, I truly didn't believe that He would send us the angel.

On November 23, 1999, I lay watching the morning sunlight as it flickered through the window shade. Right away, I noticed that Joan had left the bedroom to check on Mother. I thought about how family life would change without our precious dad. We were also comforted by the thought that soon he would join Danny in heaven.

Suddenly like a flash of lighting, an awesome presence filled the bedroom. I sensed this presence like rushing waters. *What in the world is going on?* I thought. Quickly, I glanced toward Dad's bed. I watched in disbelief as an angel lingered over Papa's bed and appeared to be caring for him.

The angel's golden hair shone brilliantly in the light around it. The angel was not of human form but seemingly moved about as if it was floating. The angel's blondish golden like hair was down to its shoulders, beautiful from the morning light through the window moving in a circle over Dad's bed.

"Dear Lord," I uttered breathlessly. *Could that be the angel I saw as a young girl?* I wondered, recalling that the angel had had golden hair. *Perhaps that is Daddy's guardian angel.* I remembered that Papa had once seen an angel while he had been sleeping in the woodlands as a young boy.

Suddenly, the angel left the bedroom. Within seconds, the angel returned. Once again, the room filled with the sound of rushing waters. *What is the angel doing now?* I wondered in disbelief. At that moment, I knew the angel was carrying Dad to the portals of heaven.

After the angel completed its divine mission, it instantly vanished from Dad's bedside. Somehow, I knew Papa had taken his last breath during the angel's second visit. Instantly, I went to embrace Dad.

Minutes later, I entered the family room. I was aware that Mom was observing Dad's bedroom from a distance. I said to Joan and Mom, "Daddy has passed beyond. Sis, I have something to tell you and Mom. God sent the angel we prayed for."

Sis gave a deep sigh and then said, "Oh, I can't believe this."

I explained how the angel had prepared Dad before his passing while the three of us embraced each other. I noticed in that moment that Mom had something on her mind. Her face filled with remarkable confidence and faith. *She's been such a strong woman her entire life,* I thought.

Mother questioned me. "Who was that blond lady visiting your dad? She was beside his bed. Why did you and Joan let her in my house so early? What was that lady doing to him?"

Joan spoke up earnestly as her brown eyes sparkled tearfully, "Sis, I can't believe what has happened. Who in the world would ever believe God answered our prayers and sent an angel?"

I admitted to Joan that I had doubted that God would send an angel. "I know exactly how you feel. We will pray and ask God to forgive our disbelief. I am glad Mama witnessed Daddy's angel," I said as my heart still jumped inside me.

About an hour later, God spoke to my heart, saying, "Oh ye of little faith."

"But Lord!" I uttered overwhelmed. Weeping, I could not imagine why God would say such a thing. Who was I kidding? Deep inside, I knew the truth. Joan and I had failed to trust the immeasurable power of the Almighty God, and that was crystal clear to both of us.

Is my faith on a wild-goose chase? I thought. Because I had not believed God would truly send an angel, was I struggling with my faith once again? I reflected upon that for a moment. Throughout the years, I had trusted that God could do all things. Now, God had revealed to me that I had doubted his faithfulness. I had a question in my heart. Was my faith strong enough to trust God to free Don from his addicted lifestyle?

"Forgive me, Lord. I am getting just what I deserve," I confessed.

Joan and I realized that God bestowed heavenly surprises on His true believers. By the angel's surprise, we had truly realized that we didn't believe God. I was heavenly inspired to believe that the angel's visit caused Joan and me to examine our hearts.

During the time of Dad's passing, Mom, Joan, and I were strengthened. Together we told Joan's pastor, who had come to pray with us, about the angel's visit.

Pastor Jones said, "I believe God sent the angel to remind this family of His faithfulness. Often in times like these, the family needs more faith. After all, it has been most difficult since Danny's death and now your father's."

Months later, I picked up my pen to write a poetic thought.

I believe
Sometime in our lives,
Angel's visit here below,
And God affirms the hour
For you and me, I know!

CHAPTER 15

MY POETRY WAS very much on my mind as I packed my suitcase. *The journey back northeast is the time to focus on writing my poetry book*, I thought.

On a bright Tuesday morning in December, I said good-bye to Mom and Joan. I told my heart not to cry. As I said good-bye, I put a smile on my face. *No, indeed, I will not cry*, I assured myself. *Be strong! Be strong!* My heart beckoned as I waited for the train. I noticed that Mother appeared terribly frail. I asked God to heal her grieving heart and our family's hearts as well.

"Mama, you and sis keep your focus on the angel's visit. That will bring comfort," I said, remembering Pastor Jones's words to the family.

"God knows we will," Joan replied. Her face was flushed by winter's cold nip.

The Blue Cardinal was on time and would make its way back to the northeast shore. I noticed right away that just about every coach was occupied. Because the Christmas season was approaching, I had expected it would be a difficult time to travel.

Minutes later, I spotted my reserved sleeper car with its wide window. Within the hour, the Great Kanawha River, which had been named by a Native American tribe (the Delaware), glimmered in the distance. How beautiful the river appeared. There were gigantic white stones, which had been smoothed by the river's merciless currents. I imagined the Delaware tribes camping beside the river, hoping to sell their handmade items to the settlers in the 1800s. *It's no wonder the Delaware called the great river A Place of White Stones*, I thought as I recalled its ancient history.

I breathed a sigh of relief and felt tears on my cheeks. It was okay. It was okay to cry now. Mama wouldn't see me.

An hour later, I reflected on my childhood memories as I heard the clinking of the train's wheels on the tracks. I pictured my mom cranking up the old Victrola to play her cherished "Kelly Waltz." I remembered her voice well. It was as soft as a nightingale's as she sang "Precious Memories" while strumming on her guitar.

The big snow sled, which had once carried our Christmas tree, would never be used again. I recalled the whispering meadows at Lewis Resort Lake. They blew sweet scents from the flowers in the early dawn. The flowing springs, which once had been so beautiful, were hidden beneath nature's wrath. I remembered all the years our children and I had spent at the farm. Times, we had waved good-bye to my parents as they had stood at the farmhouse door.

In those thoughts, I truly realized that when the things we love are no longer there, the heart welcomes precious memories. As I reminiscenced on those blissful days, the big Kanawha River vanished from sight hours later.

My fourteen joyful hours on the Cardinal did not disappoint me. It had been more than two months since I had seen Don and the kids. Dean and our daughter-in-law, Rena, had decorated the house beautifully for Christmas. Hundreds of tiny white lights covered the roof of the house for my special homecoming. Precious Kateri had embellished the house with holly scent. The Christmas tree waited to be adorned with my antique collectible bulbs.

I was caught up in the moment and was stargazing as lights lit up the night sky. My eyes filled with tears as my heart overflowed. "Thanks for loving me so much. My goodness, all of you must have decorated for weeks," I commented with my voice alive in excitement.

With his voice blustering, Dean spoke. "Dearest Mom, you always wanted the roof decorated for Christmas. We have all done our very best. Thanks to Dad for all the lights," he informed me, laughing proudly.

Minutes later, Don nodded and surrendered his thoughts. "Thank heavens, you're home at last. It has been a terrible two months without you," Don said while squeezing my hand. "Princess took good care of me," he remarked proudly.

I did not doubt Don had missed me. Perhaps emotionally and spiritually, my absence had been good for him. However, my heart confirmed that it wouldn't change a thing. Time and time again, Don had drunk excessively without me. I had learned that love came in marvelous ways through the eyes of an addicted spouse.

I realized, not all addicted people loved as deeply, as Don loved his family. I was mindful of Scripture. Apostle Paul says, "And now abide faith, hope, love, these three; but the greastest of these *is* love" (1 Cor. 13:13 NKJV).

For the remainder of the week, December's wind swirled outside as my heart wondered after thirty-seven years, why God had not freed Don from his addiction. *Why, God, have you not answered my prayers?* I asked with a grateful heart.

It was time for the Keeton feast, which I had prepared for the holiday season. We had spent many years together on Christmas. Don's loving family was my family, and I felt dearly loved by all of them.

Don's family arrived at noon. Don's sister Kay shared the miracle of God's grace healing her cancer as her husband, Richard, smiled joyfully. The doctor gave Kay only a few months to live, but God had healed Kay's cancer five times. Doris and her husband, John, brought their homemade fruitcake. Don's sister Shirley would arrive from California for Kateri and Eric's wedding, which was planned for October of 2009.

The family noticed right away that Don was seriously failing in health. Don wanted to lose weight for Kateri's wedding. Our family doctor had warned Don not to have LAP-BAND surgery. Don decided to chance the surgery. He had been preparing six months for it.

The next morning, I listened quietly to Don talking to someone in the den. *Who is he talking to?* I wondered as I switched the light on at 3:30 a.m. Don always slept with his TV on most of the night, but it was off. I continued to listen to Don for about five minutes.

I awoke at 8:30 a.m. and then noticed that Don was waiting patiently for breakfast. I was hesitant to say a word about listening to his conversation. I poured Don a cup of coffee and put it before him. Don's face grew strangely stern and with a raspy voice, he said, "I certainly had a rough night."

"What happened?" I asked.

"I thought for sure that my life was over," Don replied as he reached for my hand. Immediately, I knew that whatever had happened to Don had been serious and wonderful.

In a dreadful way, Don spoke again. "I know God spared my life last night. I promised Him that if He would let me live, I'd never drink another drop of liquor as long as I lived," Don confessed humbly with his German and English pride.

Don had been talking to God the night before. I could not wait to express my thoughts. "Well, it seems the Lord got your attention. Honey, you're so blessed. God has watched over you for more than thirty-seven years. You allowed your foolish drinking to deceive you from the God you once served," I said to Don.

I had more to say. At last, my day had come, and I would not miss this moment in time. "Don, you know that God's love is everything in this world. The point is, Don, He had to get your attention or you would have never stopped drinking. I believe that last night, God gave you a second chance at life," I said to him with a pleasing smile.

A calmness covered Don's face. "Yes, I know I'm a lucky man. Right now, I pray we can put the past behind us. This I promise you: You'll never see me drink again. You can trust me on that. I am afraid God will take me next time," remarked Don with a fearful look on his face. I smiled back, realizing God had given Don authentic peace with sobriety overnight.

My immeasurable perseverance had been worth it because I knew that Don loved God. The twelve years that followed Don's near-death experience was amazing. Not once did Don drink spirits after God's visit with him. Not once did he desire to drink alcohol. I reflected that Don' recovery was a sudden miracle after drinking so many years.

Once again, God gave Don a spirit-filled life of faith. I was so grateful to God that Don never had even one withdrawal symptom mentally. Most alcoholics who have been alcoholics that many years have a profound physiological withdrawal when stopping. We know that alcoholism affects the heart, brain, liver, mouth, pancreas, and the entire immune system.

CAROLYN L. KEETON

After Don's near-death experience, I hoped he would tell me how sorry he was for putting us through years of heartache. I waited, but he did not tell me. Don spoke softly and then louder. "What can I say that I haven't already said before?" he asked me as he blinked his eyes.

I looked Don directly in the eyes. Somehow, I knew he was sorry for the years he had abused our love.

Don let me know his feelings. "No, we cannot turn back the hand of time, but we can move forward with our lives. Is there any love in your heart left for me?" he asked, staring at me and hoping that I would respond.

The only sound in the room was the ticking of the antique clock on the wall. I hesitated to answer before we continued our conversation. A deep compassion filled my heart. I did have something to say. "Don, I know that you know God is love. It has been by God's love that I have been able to love you. It was because of God's love throughout the years of your drinking that I was able to forgive you."

Don stared at me for a few minutes. At that moment, I felt that Don's addiction had been like a daydream to him. *Daydreams let us think life is perfect, but they are not real. Daydreams are fantasy thoughts, a fool's paradise, and a dream of vain hope,* I thought.

At that moment, I realized that Don had seen himself living as a normal human being. That is the way addiction is. To Don, the years of heartache simply did not exist. Don's denial led him to believe that he had been a good dad and a loyal husband.

At last, I understood. Don saw himself as a companion who had always been responsible in every way. What an iron-hearted denial Don had lived, and at that moment, all I could feel was the deepest pity for him.

Don squirmed in his big chair like a child trying to behave. I recalled how madly in love we once had been. He had been a handsome man who had felt the world must be ruled with love, and I had agreed.

Indeed, I certainly deserved an apology from Don. Delightedly, a kiss on each cheek was his way of saying he was sorry. Then I heard a whisper within my heart that said, "Be kind to one another."

God's whispers brought peace to my deserved apology. With heart and soul, God let me know that I shouldn't judge Don for living in denial of his addiction.

I gave God thanks for letting me feel love again. I was grateful to have learned that forgiveness is *forever* and was a personal choice in our lives. In my brokenness, I learned that God's grace was sufficient for us, whatever might come in life. I asked God to bless Don even though he had betrayed our love. I thanked God that our children loved their dad dearly. They had loved him throughout the years and had never carried bitterness toward him.

During June 2008, Don's twelve years of sobriety had been like when we had first fallen in love. Unfortunately, he had many gruesome effects from his years of alcoholism. Edema, the accumulation of fluid, filled Don's body like the doctors had never seen before.

Like millions who fight alcoholism with edema, Don's years of drinking had already damaged bodily organs. Sadly, millions face death's door before giving up alcohol. I felt that Don's soul was finally desperate enough to ache for God's love, forgiveness, and protection once again. Often, such a choice does not come soon enough for addicted love ones.

There is much more in this life than fairy-tale endings. Truthfully, life is all about making a personal commitment. When we serve and love the Lord, we have his mercy and grace. I believe that is the hope each of us has with or without addictions.

Presently, a Scripture reflects my victory: "Charm *is* deceitful and beauty *is* passing, But a woman *who* fears the LORD, shall be praised" (Prov. 31:30 NKJV).

On New Year's Eve in 2008, I sat watching the fire log burning as my thoughts united with each spark. Indeed, I had learned to serve the Lord with reverence and fear. I had grown closer to the Lord's abiding love through my heartaches.

Sometimes, God takes his time healing us. When God chooses not to heal us, He has a specific purpose for our lives. I know this: "Yes, and all who desire to live godly in Christ Jesus will suffer persecution" (2 Tim. 3:12 NKJV).

CAROLYN L. KEETON

By the fire log, I reflected on the years I had cried out to God—a God who had known my heart as I had tried to survive Don's addiction. Through heartaches, we learn that true happiness is a choice we make, but there is a priceless command with it. Jesus said, to the pharisee lawyer: *"You shall love the LORD your God with all your heart, with all your soul, and with all – your mind.* This is the first and great commandment"* (Matt. 22: 37-38 NKJV).

Hours later, the fire log was slowly burning out. Only the embers in the hearth remained. I thought about all the families that drug and alcohol had destroyed, turning lives into ashes. What a comfort to know, that God's all-surpassing power can heal wounded lives.

It is impossible to articulate the beauty of God's grace, I thought. The flowers bloomed, the stars twinkled, and the mountains and the barren deserts were alive by the breath of His love.

"Well, God, here I am," I uttered as I waited for the new year to come. Another year had gone by, and soon, 2009 would burst into the heavens.

I watched from the window as the celebration at Rockford Mansion lit up the night sky. The icy wind howled as I opened the door for a closer look. I did not want to miss even one rocket being shot off. What an awesome sight. I watched the last rocket burst forth, and then winter's gusty night was silent.

Minutes later, I paused at the doorway of Don's den. It was just like him to be asleep. I shouted, "Happy New Year, sweetheart. Wake up! You missed seeing the fireworks."

Don was snoring, but I got his attention. "Don't shout at me. You are deafening my ears," Don remarked, smiling his magnificent smile.

I looked at Don and realized that he was the man I had once known. I could feel his eyes watching me and his love all around me. At that moment, I would have never imagined that on June 13, 2009, Don would face death.

Don had contracted sepsis after a second bowel eruption and had been hospitalized in ICU for more than seven weeks. Though not befitting, a doctor phoned to inform me that Don had no brain activity at all and had passed away. Dean picked me up, and we went to

Southwest, Newark Hospital to meet Kateri. The Keeton family arrived later. After the Keeton family spent time alone with Don, Kateri, Dean, and I entered Don's room.

As we entered, I felt God's presence as I had never before in my life. Right away, we noticed that Don was packed in ice. Suddenly, the Holy Spirit whispered through me, "Touch him and pray."

I thought, *Lord, what will Dean and Kateri think about praying for their dad who has already died?* Suddenly, I felt my hand lifting from the rail supernaturally to touch Don. Instantly, he opened his eyes and smiled at the three of us.

"Hello, love! Oh, I am so glad to see all of you. How are you doing, son? Princess, how are you and Eric?" he asked smiling radiantly. The three of us, in disbelief, were seeing a miracle before our eyes.

The doctors and nurses were amazed. It was so shocking, the hospital staff and doctors gave Don a new name—Lazarus—that very day.

That night when I was alone, the Holy Spirit revealed to me why Don was alive. Don wanted to renew his faith and to be baptized before he died. God's amazing grace had answered our prayers.

Don's edema fluid was severe. The doctor that operated on Don informed me that he removed seventeen pints of fluid from Don's body and had to place buckets nearby to catch it.

After Don's baptism a week later on June 13, 2009, we brought him home for Father's Day. Before dawn and beside Don's bed, I realized he was comatose. The ambulance took him once again to a nearby city hospital.

At the hospital, the doctor transferred Don to the fifth floor so that we could have family time during his passing. At 9:20 a.m., Dean, Kateri, and I entered the room. I felt God's presence as though He was waiting for us there. I noticed the window was open in the room. *This is somewhat strange,* I thought. Then suddenly, a songbird began warbling.

Dean looked at me. "Oh, where's the bird? Is it okay, Mom? I guess the bird will find its way out the window. I'll just leave it open for now," Dean remarked as he searched for the bird in the room.

Suddenly the songbird sang louder and louder. I whispered to Don, "Honey, Windy has come to sing for all of us today." No, it was not

Windy's tunes. I only said those words to Don because he loved Windy so much.

Dean remarked, "I can't find the bird. Could it possibly be a broken pipe singing? I'm sure it's a bird somewhere." I didn't know why later, that God brought to my mind the *legend* of the Thornbird by the songbird's sharp tunes. The Thornbird makes loud sharp tones, as it is dying while pressing its breast to the thorn.

The staff looked around for the bird but found no reason for the room to be filled with the piercing, sharp trills of a songbird. The hospital found no songbird, and we were in wonderment with grief.

A half hour later, Don took his last breath. Instantly, the songbird stopped singing, and the room was silent. A week later, the Department of Defense provided a military funeral with full honors for Don.

During February of 2019 while sitting by the firelog, I remembered the years of God's faithfulness. How I had survived Don's addiction for thirty-seven years? I reflected it was by God's undeserving grace. He had given me patience and endurance for thirty-seven years of Don's addiction. God had given me calmness after our children had been born so that they would never see fights or bitter quarrels between Don and me. God's grace had intervened in Don's life and had given him a miracle—a renewal of a saving salvation through Jesus Christ.

Sometimes, it takes heartaches for the soul to know God's gift of salvation. Sometimes, we must have heartaches to gain faith in Jesus Christ. Sometimes, it takes heartaches for the heart to love again. Sometimes, it takes heartaches to fully give away our love to God, I thought during Don's passing.

Sitting by the firelog, I recalled the words of my friend Shelia today: "One day at a time." How true this is. God desires that we live one day at a time, and fully rely on Him in everything we hope to achieve in our lives.

Alone in April's dawn 2019, I made a promise to finish my edits. The Westminister clock chimed at the midnight hour. A thought, of chimes in larger churches visited my heart, that chime so beautifully up to the fifth and sixth bars, and then chime out "I know that My Redeemer Liveth."

I uttered, "Lord thank you that you live in our hearts. Thank You, for giving a simple country girl's heart a story to share, so others may know your amazing grace."

Minutes later, I was inspired to write a poem for my readers, for people in drug and alcohol recovery support groups, for those in the substance abuse recovery programs at Teen Challenge USA worldwide, and for families who are enduring addictions.

Song for the Heart!

O God, we lift our *hearts* to Thee,
Here in life's enduring race.
You are a haven in life's storms,
And blessings of Thy loving grace.
O God, clothe us with loving-mercy,
For each of us, have a cross to bear.
Still, our hearts shall cleave to Thee,
And give ev'ry heartache in prayer.
O God, where valleys we walk are darkest,
Lighten our pathways in dismay.
Oh, give our *hearts* true faith in Thee,
With a ***Song*** each new born day!

CPSIA information can be obtained
at www.ICGtesting.com
Printed in the USA
BVHW031031160519
548478BV00004B/33/P